"Sebastian Gorka is one of the clearest, most consistent, and most eloquent defenders and explainers of the Trump phenomenon—and he has played that role with courage and good humor despite being vilified and slandered by the Left. Here, he uses that experience to throw light on the current battle for our culture and delivers a work of insight and encouragement for everyone who wants to see America rediscover its founding ideals."

—ANDREW KLAVAN

"In this spirited defense of the Trump presidency, administration veteran Sebastian Gorka connects the illegitimate progressive efforts to abort the Trump presidency to a larger and multifaceted elite project of transforming America into something that the Founders never intended and most Americans simply do not want. Gorka will have none of it—and he offers a lively invitation to join him in saying NO."

—VICTOR DAVIS HANSON

"Dr. Sebastian Gorka knows a thing or two about taking on totalitarians. And now, with *The War for America's Soul*, he teaches you how to do the same with the radicalized Left. This book is a strategic battle guide for how to wage the culture war in America and ensure victory in 2020 and beyond."

—KATIE PAVLICH

THE WAR FOR AMERICA'S SOUL

SEBASTIAN
GORKA

THE WAR FOR AMERICA'S SOUL

REGNERY
PUBLISHING
A Division of Salem Media Group

Regnery® is a registered trademark of Salem Communications Holding Corporation

Cataloging-in-Publication data on file with the Library of Congress

ISBN 978-1-62157-940-3
ebook ISBN 978-1-62157-963-2

Published in the United States by
Regnery Publishing
A Division of Salem Media Group
300 New Jersey Ave NW
Washington, DC 20001
www.Regnery.com

Manufactured in the United States of America

10 9 8 7 6 5 4 3 2 1

Books are available in quantity for promotional or premium use. For information on discounts and terms, please visit our website: www.Regnery.com.

Dedicated to every Patriot who helped take back America by voting for a total outsider on November 8, 2016
M.A.G.A.

CONTENTS

FOREWORD

By Dennis Prager

I had never heard the name Sebastian Gorka until I came across it in the *Forward*, a left-wing newspaper. Ever since I was a graduate student of Communist Affairs at the Russian Institute of Columbia University's School of International Affairs, I have always read the left. At that time, I regularly read *Pravda*, the Soviet Communist newspaper. After graduate school, I read English language equivalents published in America. One of the earliest and most important revelations of my life was that there was essentially no difference between *Pravda*'s positions and those of the left in the United States—on America, the world, and just about every other topic.

To this day, I read left-wing journals and writers at least as much as I do conservative journals and writers. That's why I regularly read the *Forward*. So, I came across a *Forward* article that asserted there was a high-ranking figure in the Trump administration with a pro-Nazi past: a man named Sebastian Gorka.

I am a Jew who has spent much of his life fighting for Jews and against antisemitism. When I was twenty-one-years-old, the Israeli government sent me into the Soviet Union to smuggle in Jewish religious items (banned, as all religious items were, by the Soviet regime), and, even more importantly, to smuggle out names of Soviet Jews who wanted to emigrate from the Soviet Union. Almost the only way Jews were allowed to leave the Soviet Union was at the personal invitation of another government, usually Israel. As a young Jew who was committed to Israel, Jews, and Judaism, had attended yeshivas until college, and who, as a bonus, spoke Hebrew and Russian, I was precisely the type of person the Israelis wanted for such an endeavor.

Upon returning to America, I immediately became a leader in the movement to save Soviet Jewry. Shortly thereafter, I wrote an introduction to Judaism (*The Nine Questions People Ask about Judaism*) that is still published and read. I also taught Jewish history at Brooklyn College, and fought antisemitism on the left and right.

I cite all this so that the reader understands how much it would disturb me as a Jew and as an American to even imagine that a pro-Nazi was serving in the highest echelons of the American government.

But I was not disturbed by the Gorka article in the *Forward*. The reason is that fifty years of reading and listening to the left has taught me that truth is not a left-wing value. Truth is a liberal value, and truth is a conservative value. But it has never been a left-wing value.

When leftists write or say anything, they do not ask themselves, "Is this true?" They ask, "Is this effective in destroying opponents?"

Nevertheless, having no information on this Sebastian Gorka, I could not counter what I assumed—but did not know how to prove—was a smear.

Then, about a month later, on March 17, 2017, the venerable *Jerusalem Post* published a masterful piece—"The 'Forward' Is Dead Wrong, Gorka Is a Defender of Israel, Jews"—that proved the *Forward* article about Gorka was a lie.

The *Jerusalem Post* authors' conclusion? "The *Forward* could not find a single shred of evidence suggesting that Sebastian Gorka has ever done or said anything even remotely antisemitic."

In fact, the authors made clear, not only were Gorka and his family not antisemitic, they were profoundly pro-Jew. I then spent a considerable amount of time on my national radio show reading from the *Jerusalem Post* and defending this man, Sebastian Gorka, against the terrible charge of antisemitism.

I did so for a number of reasons:

First, I was taught from a very young age something every yeshiva-graduate knows by heart—the Talmudic moral principle, "Whoever humiliates his neighbor in public, it is as if he murdered him." It was drummed into me that God regards the smearing of a human being's name as a form of murder. That's why I have tried never to do this in thirty-five years as a radio talk show host. It is why, for example, during the Clinton presidency, I forbade callers from telling a Monica Lewinsky joke on my show. She, too, is created in God's image, I kept reminding my listeners.

Second, aside from outright Holocaust-denial, as pure an evil as I know of, nothing cheapens the Holocaust and Nazism as much as falsely using the labels "Nazi" and "antisemite." If decent people are Nazis and antisemites, then Nazism and antisemitism aren't so bad.

Third, I have a visceral hatred of lies. More than any other awful thing, a lie makes evil possible—indeed, inevitable. This is a major reason why it is so important to fight the left.

Sometime later, I received a message from Sebastian Gorka, movingly thanking me for defending him. I had no idea he even knew I had done so. And he has frequently done so ever since in speeches and on his radio show. This has deeply touched me. And that, too, has a reason. In a lifetime devoted to issues of good and evil, I have concluded that gratitude is the mother of goodness. Grateful people are almost always decent people, and the ungrateful are almost always awful people. (That is another reason the left is so destructive: it promotes ingratitude. In fact, it could not exist without it.)

Sebastian Gorka loves America. Many conservatives and liberals do. The left loathes it. That's why they want to "fundamentally transform" it, as candidate-for-president Barack Obama announced five days before the 2008 election. By definition, one does not love what or whom one seeks to fundamentally transform. If your spouse wants to fundamentally transform you, he or she doesn't love you.

But unlike many other conservative and liberal Americans who love America, Sebastian Gorka understands the left's threat, that it poisons everything it touches—art, music, universities, high schools, the sexes and their relationship to one another, marriage, America, Europe, Judaism, Christianity, football, women's soccer, and even late night television shows.

I divide good people into three groups: fighters, those who help the fighters, and those who do nothing. The latter is the biggest of the three, while the first is the smallest. Sebastian Gorka is, of course, in the first category.

He loves America because, among other things, he loves liberty. He knows from the terrible pain of his own family's experiences with Nazism and communism how precious and fragile freedom is. And he understands better than most the imminent danger posed to our freedom by the left.

That's why he needs to be heard and read.

Dennis Prager is the president of the internet-based Prager University, which garners a billion views a year, the majority by viewers under thirty-five year of age. He is a nationally syndicated radio show host and columnist. His most recent book is the second volume of The Rational Bible, *his five-volume commentary on the* Torah.

WHAT THE LEFT HAS WROUGHT

Connecticut is not known for its reliably pleasant weather. As one of New England's six constituent states, its winters are bleak and gray, and its summers very often wet. So in the Gorka family preparations for our oldest child's May graduation from Trinity College in Hartford, we hoped for the best, but prepared for a rainy day in the mud. We needn't have.

When we arrived at the campus, it was a truly beautiful day. There were hundreds of chairs lined up in rows on the grass in front of the grand graduation stage on one side of the quad. Down the hill from the quad, there were dozens of marquee tents for the newly minted alumni and their loved ones to celebrate under after receiving their diplomas. It all looked most impressive and celebratory. Yet I had mixed feelings.

Of course, I was overwhelmingly proud of our daughter. Thanks to her grades, she would be graduating summa cum laude and a member of Phi Beta Kappa, America's most prestigious honor society, founded in 1776. But her academic achievements were not the main reason for our inordinate pride. Instead, it was her unbelievable work ethic, her indomitable spirit, and most of all, the way she had handled great hardship.

In addition to being an A student, our Julia was an athlete. She started rowing in high school and eventually became co-captain of her crew team at Trinity, which meant that along with the brutal 5:00 a.m. training sessions, she had to manage all the drama that attends a female sporting community at college. On top of her responsibilities with the team and her studies, she took on multiple jobs: as a manager at the college coffee shop, as a teaching assistant for four of her professors, and as a tutor at the Trinity Writing Center, helping struggling students with their papers. Not only was she establishing herself as an independent young woman with an innate desire for financial independence, she was serving others. Then there was the accident.

One of the student houses was to hold a celebration for the new school year, and Julia was invited. It was one of those rare days of decent weather in Hartford, so the festivities were moved out onto the three decks attached to the three floors of the building. Just as Julia stepped out onto the top deck, thirty feet up, the whole structure came away from the wall. The deck she was on pancaked onto the two lower decks, which were also populated with celebrating students. The result was thirty young men and women broken and distraught, entangled in the ruins of the deck structure. Soon thereafter, after first responders had taken her to the Emergency Room, we received the dreaded call from our daughter: "I'm in hospital. There's been an accident."

The truly incredible thing was that not one student died. Julia's close friend had been on the bottom deck and was in the gravest condition with multiple broken bones and fractures, including her hip. It easily could have been far worse, as the decks had been illegally constructed and weren't properly anchored to the building, despite being college property. Julia had no bones broken but had severely injured one leg—her knee and ankle—with nerve damage along most of her thigh. As a result, she wouldn't row for at least a season. And that's not to mention the psychological effects of losing all sense of safety as she felt the deck collapse under her and saw her friends fall thirty feet to the ground and land on top of each other. But incredibly she would not allow this awful experience to slow her down in any way. Not for a moment.

We suggested that she come home for a season, recuperate with us, and then go back to school when she was physically and psychologically ready. But no. She stayed at Trinity and persevered, despite having to use crutches to get from class to class. She is a truly incredible young woman. But her hard times were not over yet.

Originally a proud theological institution, Trinity has gone the way of most institutions of higher learning in America and Europe. Instead of focusing on the values, traditions, and history of our great Western civilization, the great works of the "dead white men" who brought us science, law, democracy, and free markets, Trinity has joined the ranks of those schools that see our Judeo-Christian heritage as being defined more by racism and misogyny than the truth.

A tiny handful of professors, however, remained undaunted by the rise of the "Gender Studies" and "Sustainability" mafia, and responded by creating a new institution at Trinity, called the Churchill Institute, the purpose of which is "to encourage, in every way possible, serious teaching, learning and scholarship about Western Civilization and to promote a vigorous discussion of its preservation and future trajectory."[1] Hardly controversial, you would think. But you'd be wrong.

Soon after its establishment, the Churchill Institute offered Julia a student fellowship to work there and run several of its projects. This would be her fourth job at the school! After much rumination, she agreed. This decision to associate with an organization that supports our national and civilizational heritage would be used against her in the weeks before her graduation on that sunny day in May.

You should know that Trinity College is home to Johnny Eric Williams, a man I refuse to dignify with the title "professor" because of his extremist views and despicable actions.

This person is meant to teach sociology to the young people attending the school. Instead he is a proud purveyor of bigotry and race-based hatred.

Famous for his pronouncements on social media, Williams has stated that simply being white is an act of "terrorism," and that "all self-identified white people (no exceptions) are invested in and collude with systemic white racism/white supremacy."[2]

Most outrageous and despicable of all was what he said after James Hodgkinson, a volunteer for the Bernie Sanders campaign, took a rifle, a handgun, and a hit-list of Republican politicians to a baseball diamond in Northern Virginia with the intent to murder as many as he could of those present at a practice for a charity game. Almost taking the life of Congressman Steve Scalise, he was killed by two brave members of the Capitol Police. Williams tweeted that the ambulance crews who rushed to the shooting should have "#LetThemF*ckingDie."[3]

Apart from a brief hiatus from teaching, this vile individual has paid no penalty for his racism or death-wish extremism. He still teaches at Trinity, with the president of the college defending him under the banner of "academic freedom." Note: Williams and the college president, Joanne Berger-Sweeney, are both black. Ask yourself what would have ensued had they both been white, and Williams had made public statements to the effect that, "Blackness is terrorism." I doubt his academic freedom would have saved him from being summarily fired, tenure or no tenure.

This last piece of the puzzle provides context for what happened next to Julia and what transpired on the day of her graduation.

A month before the big day, the Churchill Institute was targeted by a small group of vocal students who managed to have it formally disapproved by the Trinity Student Government. Why? Well, because the Churchill Institute's mission—"to encourage, in every way possible, serious teaching, learning and scholarship about Western Civilization"—celebrates the values upon which America and the West were built, and so challenges the ideology of "identity politics" and victimhood that are the bedrock of left-wing politics and academe today. And because she was associated with the Institute, our daughter Julia came under attack as well. Just before her graduation, a social media campaign was launched against Julia, using her name and picture, and posters were placed around campus stating: "This is the face of Racism. This is the face of White Supremacy."

Imagine this happening to your daughter. Imagine this happening to you, as a young person in college. Imagine this happening to someone, like my daughter, who not only doesn't have a racist fiber in her being, but who, as part of her law and policy studies in school, focused explicitly on helping the most disadvantaged women—often minority women—who are abused and end up financially destitute thanks to the actions of their reprobate husbands or partners. Leftist activists aimed their hatred at Julia just days before her graduation—and what did the school do? Nothing.

I contacted Trinity College president Berger-Sweeney to express my concerns and highlight the protection she had afforded an avowed bigot on her faculty, Johnny Eric Williams, and I contrasted that with the utter lack of response to the harassment Julia had received. She replied with a noncommittal email full of empty liberal nostrums. Since then, I found out that the campus police had almost immediately identified the students behind the hate campaign, but when the culprits' left-wing credentials became known to the school, one of the deans forced the officer in charge to quietly drop the whole investigation. Apparently, "social justice" doesn't apply to conservatives.

Now we come to the graduation on that beautiful sunny day on the quad of Trinity College.

Though I'm not known for being the "touchy-feely" sort, I was unusually anxious as our daughter's graduation approached. My time in the White House working for President Trump had seen a barrage of hate launched against us, with the press attacking not only me, my wife, and my high-school son—whom the *Forward* described as a "traitor" in the headline of one of its dozens of hit pieces on me and my family—but also the good name of my late mother. The last thing I wanted to do was attract negative attention to myself from within a large crowd attending the graduation at a decidedly leftist school and in any way lessen the sense of achievement and celebration that Julia had every right to revel in.

So instead of sitting in the crowd with my wife, my mother-in-law, and my sister-in-law, I found a spot in the shade next to a large oak, just off to one side, from where I could see the stage but no one could see me. Perfect. I could watch the events unfold and photograph Julia as she came up to the stage, and then we could all move directly to our tent to celebrate with her, her friends, and their parents. But as an old Hungarian saying goes: "Man may plan, but God implements."

On the way to my special spot I had to walk past a group of other Trinity parents. Several made eye contact, and I saw that flicker which translates as: "Don't I know you?" There I was thinking I was being so smart, so subtle and discrete—but for naught. I needn't have worried. The gentlemen stood up as I passed, asked me my name and then proceeded to shake my hand and thank me for what I do. Then the parents of one of Julia's friends, a lovely couple from Ireland, saw me in my secluded spot and came right over. They, as legal immigrants, regarded me as a fellow legal immigrant made good, and were also admirers of my old boss, the president, and we chatted right up until the ceremony began. My attempt to be inconspicuous was failing and we hadn't even begun the official part of the day.

There were several addresses from the stage—by the president of the school; the senior dean; the guest of honor, Samuel Kennedy, president and chief executive officer of the Boston Red Sox; and one of the students—followed by special awards, before the hundreds of graduating students received their diplomas.

For the record, Kennedy's speech was unusually good for a commencement address, peppered with personal anecdotes from his time at Trinity and tales of his perseverance over the decades before he became the recognized success he is today and brought success to the Red Sox. This was very refreshing, especially given that he even mentioned President Trump's name without a hint of any negativity. I cannot say the same for the student speech.

The girl who gave the address on behalf of the graduating students could have come right out of central casting at Democrat party headquarters, a veritable mini Alexandria Ocasio-Cortez. Her whole speech—this coming from a successful white girl at a prestigious school full of the progeny of wealthy, middle- and upper-class families—was about one thing: sexism, which she deemed the greatest problem our nation faces today. More important than jihadi terrorism, more important than the 100,000 illegal immigrants crossing our borders each month, more important than human trafficking, more important than the 72,000 deaths last year in the United States from drug overdoses, more important than China's bid to displace America as the world's leading superpower.

As an indication of just how effective the Left's indoctrination has become, let me recount some of the worst nuggets of her address.

She regaled her captive audience with her story of attending the Women's March, where she saw a t-shirt that read, "The Future Is Female," which led her to wax lyrical about how that sentiment was tantamount to surrender, that instead we need to shout from the rooftops, "Make the Present Female!" The fact that the original statement is, in and of itself, a sexist demand was utterly lost on her, as was the irony of her demanding that the here and now be the exclusive domain of only one half of mankind. And this is not to mention the sheer irrationality of designating a sex to the past, present, or future. Her contribution to feminist progress—something she described about a dozen times as her "call to action!"—was the placement of "Green Dot" decals around campus to "raise awareness." This is not parody, dear reader. This actually happened.

One can smile and laugh, but this asinine speech is evidence of a deeper, more serious, problem.

First, the obvious one: instead of understanding just how free and empowered she is, standing at a podium, giving the student address at her college graduation, she wants to claim victim status. Just how brainwashed does a twenty-two-year-old adult have to be to believe that America is riven by sexism? America is not exactly the febrile vision from *The Handmaid's Tale* that she wishes us to believe it is.

And how ignorant and closed-minded must you be to lecture Americans on the sexism in our country, ignoring entirely those nations and cultures where sexism is a real problem? She didn't spend one second discussing the plight of women in the Middle East, especially in theocratic Muslim regimes such as Saudi Arabia, Pakistan, or Iran, where "honor crimes" are a horrific reality, and a woman can be beaten or killed by the state for wearing the wrong attire or loving the wrong person. No. Women's rights in Connecticut are the problem.

In the middle of all these speeches, I had to get up and stretch my legs. As soon as I did, two officers from the college police department started walking my way. What now? I needn't have worried. They wanted to say hello and asked to take a selfie before they radioed their superior to come say hi. He did and introduced me to his team which included former FBI agents, Connecticut state police, and Hartford police department veterans. Before he had to say goodbye, he took the time to rush back to his office and return with patches from each department as a souvenir. I would share what these great men told me about life as cops at a school dominated by political correctness, but I do not wish to endanger their livelihoods.

By now, the conferral of degrees was about to start, so I found a spot where I could see Julia as she approached the stage and take a picture to memorialize her great achievements. The officers had shared with me that they knew what had happened to her and said they were ready, and I trusted them. Julia was beaming as she walked up, and I was greatly relieved when she took her diploma from the president without there being any disturbance from those who had targeted her so vilely over the last few weeks.

We listened to Trinity's female "reverend" give the final invocation without ever once mentioning our Savior, Jesus Christ—this at an institution founded by none other than Bishop Thomas Brownell as a home for Christian learning—and then it was time for the new graduates to throw their caps in the air and to celebrate four long years of academic and athletic achievement. I found my way back to our party, and we reconnected with Julia. In the crush, I became slightly separated from the rest of the group. A young woman walked up to me, stretched out her hand, and said: "Are you Sebastian Gorka, the Sebastian Gorka who worked for Donald Trump in the White House?" I smiled and said, "Yes, that's me!" To which she responded: "Well then FUCK OFF, you Nazi!"

She did this in front of other families, other parents—witnesses all—and then walked away.

I was momentarily taken aback. This was not the first time since I joined the Trump administration that someone had been publicly obscene to my face. But usually it's done by a coward who sees me on the street, rolls down the window of his car, and shouts something vulgar as he drives by. This was face to face, at a college graduation ceremony.

After I gathered myself and saw where she had gotten to, I decided that this demanded a response. I walked up to her and the two ladies she was with (probably her mother and grandmother). The girl wasn't wearing an academic gown, so she wasn't a graduating student, but likely the sister of one of the graduates. I said to her: "Just who do you think you are? My parents suffered as children under the Nazis, and then my father was tortured and imprisoned by the secret police. And you have the temerity to call me a 'fucking Nazi?'"

At this point the woman who was likely her mother looked at the girl and said: "Did you really say that to this man?" With a chilling rictus grin on her face, she proudly admitted that she had. I said, "You know nothing about me, who I am, or what I believe. You are a brainwashed useful idiot, and it's people like you who helped ensure that the trains ran on time into the death-camps."

This incident should deeply concern all Americans who love this country.

I've been told I can be imposing. I'm six-foot-four, 260 pounds, and a former rugby and judo enthusiast. That a slip of a girl could be so brainwashed that she could angrily get up in my face as she did, where she did, is an indication that the Left have perfected their tools of indoctrination so as to instill irrational levels of hatred in our young people, hatred that they are prepared to act upon. This reality endangers all of us who believe that we live in the greatest nation ever created by man.

If we fail to understand just how the Left achieved all this in the span of less than fifty years, we run the risk of losing the next election and surrendering our future to the control of those who will rule through hate and wish to dismantle and destroy all that we hold dear.

This book will help you understand how the Left has accomplished all that they have accomplished, the incredible threat they pose, and what it will take to win against them in 2020.

CHAPTER ONE

OBAMAGATE: THE ATTEMPTED COUP AGAINST DONALD J. TRUMP

C oup d'état is not a phrase to be used lightly.

Unless you are an uber-iconoclastic strategic thinker and author like Ed Luttwak who built his career, in part, by authoring the book, *Coup d'État: A Practical Handbook*, this is not a topic to joke about or to trifle with, as it conjures images of bloody takeovers by juntas in banana republics, or of tanks barricading parliament buildings in Moscow in the 1990s.

It is not a word that we associate with our Republic, where the Constitution and the rule of law are paramount. But a coup d'état is exactly what the Democrat party and the Obama administration attempted against Donald J. Trump both during his candidacy and after he took office as president.

At first, few took seriously Donald Trump's announcement that he was running for president. The media and political elite were certain that the candidacy of the blond billionaire from New York—the star of his own reality TV show with the catchphrase *"You're fired!"*—was absurd; it was written off by many as a publicity stunt. The establishment's disdain for Donald Trump was captured perfectly in one moment on that egregiously offensive show *Real Time with Bill Maher*. In June 2015, Maher asked Ann Coulter which of the Republican candidates was the most likely to win. When she answered: "Donald Trump!" the panel (Maher, liberal Joy Reid, Never-Trumper Matt Lewis, and Democratic politician Luis Gutiérrez) guffawed, and the audience burst out laughing like trained circus animals.[1] But then, slowly but surely, candidate Trump whittled away at the other sixteen establishment GOP candidates to become the Republican nominee. This was, to the establishment, an inconceivable turn of events. Trump was not a part of the political class. He wasn't beholden to special interests. He had no ties to the oil industry, tobacco, or Big Pharma. And, what was worse, he was a "rube." In a choice between vichyssoise and a Big Mac, he'd go for the burger. In a choice between watching Charlie Rose or Sean Hannity, Trump watched the FOX News host. In a choice between joining the bipartisan consensus of the Washington swamp or putting America first, well there was no question. Therefore, this man had to be stopped.

As I write this book, a new attorney general has been unleashed upon the conspirators behind what I have called Obamagate. For two years, the Department of Justice was run by the well-meaning, but out of his depth Jeff Sessions, former United States senator from Alabama. Sessions allowed the Obama Era Deep-State holdovers to convince him to recuse himself from overseeing the Russia "collusion" investigation when there was no need for him to do so.[2] In William Barr, his successor, we finally have someone at the helm who knows what he is doing, has a spine made of rebar, and who has made it his mission to root out corruption.

Already, in his multiple appearances before Congress and in a handful of lengthier media interviews, Attorney General Barr has made it clear that he is on the warpath, that he is not satisfied with the contradictory answers he has received to questions he has asked about surveillance operations undertaken by the Obama Era FBI, Department of Justice, CIA, and other elements of the American intelligence and law enforcement establishment.[3] And to that end, in addition to ongoing inspector general investigations, he has tasked the U.S. attorney for Connecticut, John Durham, to look into just how the "Russia Collusion" investigation began and with what predication.[4] Durham is a man who has dedicated a large part of his life to investigating and prosecuting bent cops.[5]

As a result, we are only at the beginning of this journey of discovery, to return our Republic to a nation defined by the rule of law. On my national radio show, *AMERICA First*, I have repeatedly asked those at the forefront of uncovering the truth about this scandal—the biggest political scandal in American history—just how much they think we know so far. Their answers concur at just 10–15 percent of all the corruption and criminality involved. Nevertheless, given the massive disinformation campaign associated with this series of crimes, the support provided by the "Fake News" "mainstream" media, and the sheer complexity and breadth of this conspiracy, I believe it to be essential for you to know as much as possible right now.

In the next few pages, I have collected as much of the truth that we now know. In this I am indebted, as we all should be as Americans, to the unstinting work of my friends and colleagues Joe DiGenova, Victoria Toensing, Sara Carter, Andy McCarthy, John Solomon, Catherine Herridge, Gregg Jarrett, Lee Smith, and especially Dan Bongino. His book *Spygate: The Attempted Sabotage of Donald J. Trump* must be read by all patriots. Additionally, the speech he gave to the 2018 David Horowitz Freedom Center Restoration Weekend is the best early summary of what we know about the conspiracy, and I am indebted in this chapter to his having given it and to his clarity when doing so.[6]

First, we must understand the context of the scandal. Without the context it is nigh impossible for a law-abiding citizen who has never seen the Clinton Crime Cartel or Team Obama operate up close to believe what these political actors and their bureaucratic agents did to our nation. We need to remind ourselves what they had already done—and were capable of—before they decided that Donald Trump was a threat and that he and anyone associated with him had to be politically and judicially neutralized.

The Fake News Industrial Complex would have you believe that the Obama years were "scandal free" and that his was the most transparent and accountable White House in the history of our country. In fact, it was the most scandal-ridden eight years of any modern presidential administration. During his tenure, Obama saw fit to use the incredible powers of the IRS to harass and target conservative Tea Party organizations.[7] (Richard Nixon had considered using the IRS to target his opponents but never actually implemented this tactic.[8] Unlike Obama.) Obama was likewise fine with using the National Park Service as a political weapon during a government shutdown, having park rangers barricade our capital's memorials so as to inconvenience our World War II veterans who had come to Washington to pay respects to their fallen comrades.[9]

Then there was the use of the Espionage Act to harass conservative journalists—a violation of freedom of the press that the mainstream media didn't care to report much about because they were too busy promoting the Obama administration's press releases. To this day we do not know the full story of just how pervasively journalists whom Obama saw as his enemies—including FOX News's James Rosen and CBS's Sheryl Atkisson—were illegally spied upon because their work was "too truthful" when it came to the crimes of the Obama White House. What we do know is that Rosen and even his elderly parents were surveilled by the federal government absent any predicate of a real crime[10] and that Atkisson's private communications and her personal computers were penetrated by individuals clearly acting in the interests of the Obama administration.[11] Add to that the fact that during the eight years of the Obama administration, more journalists and their sources were prosecuted and imprisoned under the Espionage Act of 1917 than by all previous presidents combined,[12] and we begin to understand the attitude to rule of law, transparency, and accountability that the former constitutional law "professor" Barack Obama had.

It was Obama's secretary of state, Hillary Clinton, who lied about the true cause of the deadly attack on our consulate in Benghazi that led to the gruesome torture and murder of Ambassador Chris Stevens and three other brave Americans.[13] In order to deflect the blame for the gruesome terror attack in the run-up to his reelection, Obama's team blamed a sophomoric YouTube video about Mohammed for inciting the murders, hiding from public sight the truth that it was al Qaeda that had staged the assault on the anniversary of September 11th and that Ambassador Stevens had repeatedly sent signals to Secretary of State Hillary Clinton that matters were escalating and that he and his people needed more security. He was ignored and sacrificed to the jihadists which the Clinton State Department and Obama White House wanted to pretend were not a serious threat.[14]

Then there was the president's unconstitutional approach to the Fourth Amendment and due process. In an attempt to make the otherwise less than manly Obama look "tough" and decisive, the White House established something called the "Threat Disposition Matrix" on a secure tablet for the 44th president. This device would hold a classified list of top, high value targets—terrorists from around the world connected to groups like al Qaeda or ISIS, with their locations when known. This is what Obama used to choose whom we would kill next via a drone strike or other action.[15]

This may seem the opposite of scandalous, since killing terrorists is a good thing, correct? Yes, it is. But first there is the absurdity of having the president of the United States make tactical decisions about which terrorist should be killed today. That is not what a president does. In World War II, Presidents Roosevelt and Truman would never have toyed with lists of which Third Reich tank commander or fighter pilot to kill next just to look "tough." But the real scandal is that this list included U.S. citizens, some of whom were chosen by Obama for assassination and then actually killed, with zero due process, in flagrant contravention of an American citizen's constitutional rights before the law.[16] One day it's Americans targeted by hell-fire missiles on foreign soil, what if next it's Americans targeted here in America, similarly without access to justice?

This was Obama's White House. From the targeting of American patriots at home via the IRS, to missile strikes killing Americans abroad without due process before the law, the Obama administration had no qualms—none—with using the incredible might of the federal government against those it did not like, or wanted to eliminate. That is how we arrive at the plot to subvert candidate Trump's campaign through the use of the Department of Justice (DOJ), FBI, CIA, and National Security Agency (NSA), for political purposes.

Let us start with the NSA. After the 9/11 attacks of 2001, the powers and capacities of the NSA grew exponentially, and this continued under the Obama administration, to the point that in 2011 the nation's premier electronic surveillance agency had to build a new data storage facility in the middle of the desert in Utah. The Obama administration spent $1.5 billion of taxpayer funds for a site that stretches over 1.5 million square feet to house up to twelve exabytes of surveilled data.[17] To understand just how gargantuan a capability that represents, U. C. Berkeley scientists estimate that five exabytes is equivalent to the amount of words all human beings have ever spoken, in all languages, since we started to use language.[18] The NSA can store more than twice that amount of classified information at just its Utah facility, and—as far as we know at the moment—this is where the crimes against Donald Trump begin.

Government officials with the requisite clearances may "query" the NSA database. Since the NSA can snoop on telephone conversations, texts, emails, radio communications, and basically any form of electronic information transmittal around the world, this allows them to "touch" anyone anywhere who has moved beyond stone tablets, papyrus scrolls, or old-school snail mail for communication and record-keeping. This is a level of power that spymasters of yore such as Cardinal Richelieu, or even Ian Fleming's fictional "M," could barely imagine.

Since the advent of the Internet has made communications truly global and practically instantaneous, the NSA can be used to target any bad guy on the web, but in doing so, the vaunted "six steps of separation" mean that one justified request for an intercept on a high value target will ensnare totally innocent people in the net of "metadata" which the NSA has at its disposal.[19] For example, the CIA or the Drug Enforcement Administration may make a request for all the available communications of a specific jihadi terrorist or a businessman running a front company for a drug cartel, and the NSA will be able to retrieve said target's emails, intercept his phone-calls, and even penetrate his hard drives should his personal computers have a connection to the Internet.[20] And of course, those communications will include thousands upon thousands of interactions with totally innocent people.[21] Terrorists and drug-runners make calls to the dentist too when they need a root-canal. They hire cars via email from reputable rental companies. They send birthday greetings to grandma. The NSA will pick up all of these communications as well, including totally innocent exchanges with American citizens who have done nothing wrong. That's why they need a twelve exabyte storage facility in Utah.

When a government official makes a justifiable request to surveil a target individual, any intercepted communication that involves an

American citizen who is not otherwise under investigation—who is not being surveilled as an individual of primary interest because he committed a crime or because there is reason to suspect that he will—must be handled in such a way that that individual's identity is "masked" or redacted within the intercepted material, so as to protect that U.S. citizen's constitutional rights.[22] There is, however, an exception.

If a senior government official is curious as to why this American's name can be connected to a person deemed a threat to national security, they can request that the person's name be revealed. This is called "unmasking" and should be invoked rarely and only if there is some valid national security justification for injuring that citizen's Fourth Amendment rights. Having spoken to senior political appointees and intelligence professionals with multiple decades of government service, I was told that if you make more than a handful of unmasking requests in your entire time in government that is highly unusual. But not for President Obama and his team. To quote Dan Bongino, former member of the NYPD and former presidential service detailee with the U.S. Secret Service:

> The Obama administration figures out that through unmasking, in other words wiretapping people, pretending they're targeting foreigners, and then querying information in this [NSA] database, that they can get all the political opposition research in the world that they need against the Trump team.[23]

And the numbers are astounding. In the last year of the Obama administration, according to PBS, hardly a rabid rightwing source, more than 1,900 Americans' identities were revealed based on these previously incredibly rare requests.[24] In just one year.

One individual alone, Obama's ambassador to the United Nations, Samantha Power, made hundreds of unmasking requests in just twelve months, almost one per working day.[25] And this by a person who has no formal position in the law enforcement or intelligence community. On what grounds does the head of our diplomatic mission to the UN need to reveal the identities of hundreds and hundreds of American citizens? This has nothing to do with the work of an ambassador or with representing American interests at the United Nations headquarters in New York. No, the reason is a political reason.

Spying directly upon members of the Trump campaign and the Trump family for political purposes during an election year is unjustifiable. But find a public event in New York where the Russian ambassador is in the same room with General Mike Flynn, or find a reception to honor the Chinese New Year that is attended by a Trump campaign adviser and the Chinese ambassador, and there you go. Target the diplomats, scoop up all the data, and then start unmasking your political opponents in the hope that you can find anything resembling dirt that Hillary Clinton and the DNC can use as opposition research to guarantee her victory in the election and so maintain the Left's grip on the White House for another eight years.

But there was a snag. Not everyone is a disciple of Saul Alinsky, author of *Rules for Radicals*, and not everyone, even in Washington, agrees with the philosophy that the ends justify the means. One man in Washington took a principled stand, and if it weren't for the director of the National Security Agency itself, we might have ended up living in a very different America. The hero of the hour was Admiral Mike Rogers.

Admiral Rogers realized that his NSA database was being queried to find information about American citizens at an unprecedented rate. He started to investigate who was doing the querying and what, if any, justification was being given to gather information from his systems, information that is meant to be used exclusively to subvert and derail the operations of terrorists and spies working for adversarial nations, not to spy on domestic political rivals of the president or the Democrat party. Admiral Rogers made his concerns known to the officials at the secret court that issues surveillance warrants against American citizens under the Foreign Intelligence Surveillance Act (FISA).[26]

Since the scandals of the Nixon years, if the DOJ or FBI wants to surveil an American on U.S. soil, a case has had to be made in front of a FISA court judge that requisite evidence exists to presume the individual concerned is collaborating, or was associated, with an enemy nation or terrorist organization and that as such the target's constitutional rights to privacy, and against unreasonable searches, can be temporarily suspended due to probable cause.[27] Rogers saw a pattern that indicated that Americans were being targeted who had no connection to America's enemies but who were simply conservatives who worked for or were associated with Hillary Clinton's rival for the highest position in the land.[28] And the situation turned out to be so egregious that after a preliminary investigation, the FISA Court issued a scathing report following the 2016 election, which included the shocking revelation that the ultra-classified NSA database of communications intercepts was being queried regularly by contractors working with the FBI, by people who weren't even government employees and had no mandate or legal authority to spy on anyone, let alone illegally reveal the identities of innocent American nationals who just happened to have been caught up in the NSA's electronic nets.[29]

But let's get back to the original conspiracy.

The elections have occurred. The woman who everyone in the media and on the Left said would win was trounced in the Electoral College. Donald Trump will be president of the United States. Thanks to the peculiar system we have developed in our nation, however, the transition of power is a very slow one. In the United Kingdom, after an election, the old prime minister starts packing straight away, and the new head of government and his cabinet officials move into power within a matter of days. In our Republic, you may win in early November, but you don't take up the reins of government for months—not until noon on January 20, when the new president takes his oath of office before the chief justice of the Supreme Court and the world.

But Admiral Rogers knew the law had been broken in a systematic conspiracy to politically target the president-elect. Before even more damage could be done during the frantic weeks while Obama's minions were still operating the levers of government and running the most powerful intelligence apparatus in the world, Admiral Rogers felt duty-bound to tell the soon-to-be 45th president that he and his people had been illegally spied upon. So ten days after the election, without telling the outgoing President Obama, or his director of national intelligence, James Clapper, Admiral Rogers traveled unheralded to New York to visit President-elect Trump and inform him that he had been targeted by Obama and his team, who had made illegal use of the NSA surveillance database to unmask people affiliated with the Trump campaign.[30]

When the soon-to-be commander in chief heard how he, his family, and his team had been illegally surveilled for months, he immediately decided to leave the compromised Trump Tower and move operations to Bedminster, New Jersey.[31] Later, President Trump went public with what he had learned, with his famous tweets about being spied upon, starting with "Terrible! Just found out that Obama had my 'wires tapped' in Trump Tower just before the victory. Nothing found. This is McCarthyism!"[32] Eventually, after Team Trump's evacuation of their New York headquarters, Obama found out that Admiral Rogers had revealed his administration's illegal activities and took action by having his people attack Rogers and call for his removal over spurious accusations related to drone strikes.[33] Rogers survived the obviously false charges. His British counterpart, however, was implicated in the Obama administration's conspiracy against Trump.

The anodyne sounding Government Communications Headquarters, or GCHQ, is the United Kingdom's signals intelligence agency, the British intelligence community's analog to the NSA. Over the last few years we have learned more and more about how John Brennan, Obama's director of central intelligence, circumvented the U.S. Constitution and used allied nations to do his dirty work of spying on American citizens for him.[34] So far, this international web includes Australia, Italy, and, most importantly, the United Kingdom.[35]

It is important to understand who John Brennan was and is. By his own admission, Brennan was a radical who voted for the Communist party candidate for president at the height of the Cold War, just four years before he interviewed to join the CIA and incredibly was allowed to join that agency. His career in intelligence was not an illustrious one. He tried to become a case officer but failed badly, ending up instead as a less than mediocre and embittered desk-jockey analyst, whose promotions—finally to acting interim director of the National Counterterrorism Center for a year—were largely a matter of seniority and political favor. After about twenty-five years at the CIA, he left to work in the private sector and cash in on his intelligence experience.[36] Then Obama pulled this former Communist sympathizer out of obscurity and made him first his deputy national security adviser for Homeland Security and Counterterrorism, and then director of the CIA, a position from where he would take revenge on the capable agents and operators whose ranks he was not fit to join, by completely reorganizing the agency and elevating analysts to positions where they could make operational decisions in a series of new functional centers he structurally imposed upon Langley.

When it became clear that Donald Trump was no longer a challenger just to be laughed at but a serious threat to Hillary Clinton's election and Barack Obama's "legacy," Brennan became the key player in the illegal conspiracy to undermine and sabotage the Trump campaign and the Trump presidency.

Again, I cannot stress enough the fact that we are still at the beginning of finding out the depth and breadth of corruption encouraged by President Obama and executed by his cabinet members and his advisers, and that the fullest accountings to date are to be found in the investigative reporting by my friends named above, and in the key books already published on Obamagate: Dan Bongino's *Spygate: The Attempted Sabotage of Donald J. Trump* and Gregg Jarrett's *The*

Russia Hoax: The Illicit Scheme to Clear Hillary Clinton and Frame Donald Trump and Andy McCarthy's *Ball of Collusion*. But for the purposes of this book, here are the major additional pieces of basic information you need to know.

Soon after Admiral Rogers decided to fight the corruption of his political masters, strange things started to occur, most significant of all, the sudden resignation "for personal family reasons" of GCHQ Director Bob Hannigan—this after a leak to the press that GCHQ had forwarded electronic intercepts of Trump campaign officials to the Obama administration. Remember: when a foreign intelligence agency is spying on U.S. citizens, they're not breaking our laws. And that's how Brennan, Clapper, and their boss, Barack Obama managed to circumvent our Constitution and the laws against political espionage targeting American citizens once they had realized that Donald Trump's candidacy for the highest position in the land wasn't so funny and outlandish an idea anymore. But this is not the full extent of their perversion of our intelligence and law enforcement communities. And here we return to the incredible powers of the FISA court.

In a childish reference to a *Rolling Stones* lyric, presumably as an inside joke since candidate Trump liked to use the *Stones'* song "You Can't Always Get What You Want" to end his rallies, the highest levels of the Obama Administration authorized *Operation CrossFire Hurricane*—a truly unprecedented exploitation of the combined counterintelligence powers of the FBI, CIA, and NSA aimed at the Trump campaign based on the accusation that the Russians had "colluded" with the Trump campaign to win the election. That accusation was ludicrous on its face, and, as we now know after three years of constant media hysteria and forty million dollars spent on the

Mueller investigation and the publication of its report, there was never any evidence to back it up.

The outrageous "collusion" accusation was based upon a "dossier" of alleged compromising "intelligence" compiled by a former British MI-6 intelligence agent named Christopher Steele.[37] Steele had excellent connections to the Kremlin and admitted to a visceral hatred of Donald Trump.[38] This man was paid millions of dollars by Hillary Clinton's lawyers and the DNC to provide a file of opposition research against Donald Trump.[39] The final product turned out to be an utter fabrication built in large part upon disinformation provided to Steele by his contacts in the Russian government. But that didn't matter to key intelligence and law enforcement officials including John Brennan, James Clapper, Loretta Lynch, James Comey, Rod Rosenstein, Andrew McCabe, and Peter Strzok, among others, who acted as Obama's praetorian guard.[40] In flagrant disregard for the rule of law, regulations on abuse of power, and perhaps perjury, the fake "dossier" file was used to obtain multiple secret FISA warrants, warrants that would allow unfettered surveillance of all the people working for or related to Donald Trump thanks to something called the "two hop rule." Here I will again quote former Secret Service agent Dan Bongino, as he explained Obama's use of this rule:

> Meaning, if I spy on you, and you're a member of the Trump team, I can hop to everybody you emailed and then everybody they emailed. So basically all I need to do is get a FISA warrant on the guy cleaning the floors in Trump Tower, and I've got everyone. Because if he emailed his boss, and his boss emailed Don, Jr., I get everybody.[41]

And that's exactly what they did.

Without any probable cause they obtained a secret warrant to spy on Carter Page, a minor figure advising the Trump campaign. Using information that was paid for by the Democrat party and the Hillary Clinton campaign, Obama's Department of Justice and the FBI applied for a warrant to spy on a man who had not only committed no crime, but as a former naval officer and Annapolis grad, had in the past confidentially assisted the FBI in catching Russian spies in the United States—I repeat, catch them, not work for them![42]

And they did all this while hiding the fact that the "intelligence" they were using to justify the illegal surveillance was in fact opposition research generated for political purposes, compiled by a foreign spy with a political agenda, and included disinformation provided by the Russian government. This is who Barack Obama and his team are. Hardened ideologues who had no compunction in using the most powerful tools of government anywhere in the Western world and conspiring with foreign agents to subvert our Constitution and our Republic. But they didn't count on the will of the American people to take back their country.

Expecting to be able to manufacture enough seemingly damaging "intelligence" against the upstart from Queens, they failed. Sixty-three million Americans chose the "wrong" candidate. According to the *New York Times* and the *Huffington Post*, on the night of the election, Hillary had a more than 92 percent chance of winning. But she lost. Despite spending $1.4 billion, despite having almost all of the media on her side, despite the fact that she was running against an outsider who had never held political office, despite the defection of the Never-Trump Republicans, she failed to win the presidency because she assumed that position was hers by right of her sex and her last name. And after weeks of openly scaremongering that Donald Trump would not accept the result of the election if he lost, it was Hillary who refused to personally concede defeat, once it was incontrovertible, sending her evil *éminence grise*, John Podesta, out instead to break the sad news to the weeping drones assembled at the Javits Center in New York. The unthinkable had happened, and it was Hillary Clinton who refused to accept it.

But now there was real trouble. If Hillary wasn't going to be president, then none of the Obama/Clinton cartel would stay in power. Donald Trump would get to place his confidantes—conservatives— into the top positions of the U.S. government, which would include naming a new attorney general, a new director of the CIA, and perhaps a new director of the FBI. No one in the Deep State had planned for this. All those who had conspired against Trump had reason to fear that the evidence of what they had been doing illegally against candidate Trump and his people might be exposed. What was to be done? The obvious answer: bring in a "fixer" to hide the truth, subvert the new administration, divert attention away from all their crimes, and generate a way to politically indict the new commander in chief. Enter Robert Mueller, former FBI director and close friend or former colleague to all those implicated in the largest political scandal in America's history. The initial idea was to get Mueller reappointed to his old position at the top of the FBI, where he could deep-six all the compromising evidence forever.

Rod Rosenstein, Mueller's former Department of Justice colleague and lackey, managed to help engineer things, and Mueller was eventually invited to the White House to meet the new president on May

16, 2017, a week after President Trump dismissed James Comey, with good reason (and Rod Rosenstein's advice), as director of the FBI. Mueller interviewed to get his old job back and thought that as a former FBI director, and one who had served under both a Republican and a Democrat president (George W. Bush and Barack Obama), he was a shoe-in. Who better qualified than someone who had done it all before, with bipartisan support? But no. President Trump saw Mueller as past his sell-by date, a man of another time and low energy, the opposite of the new commander in chief. President Trump decided, "Thanks, but no thanks. We need fresh blood."

For the conspirators, the question then became: how to cover up the hundreds of illegal unmaskings, the unjustifiable NSA database queries, and the unsubstantiated secret FISA warrants? There was only one answer: Mueller had to be made so powerful he could bring down the new president, and that's exactly what the de facto acting attorney general Rod Rosenstein decided to make happen. Remember, by this time, the real attorney general, Jeff Sessions, had, on the advice of Obama holdovers, taken the fatal decision to recuse himself from anything to do with Russia investigations because he had met the Russian ambassador at a public function during the campaign and forgotten to tell Congress that he had done so during testimony.[43] As a result, his deputy, swamp-dwelling survivor *par excellence*, Rod Rosenstein, became, to all intents and purposes, the actual attorney general on matters related to Russia. Rosenstein failed to get Mueller appointed as director of the FBI, but now he could go one better: he could make Mueller a special counsel to investigate the sitting president.[44]

Remarkably, less than twenty-four hours after Mueller failed so egregiously in his interview with President Trump, his friend Rosenstein called him back to Department of Justice headquarters and made him the most powerful prosecutor in the world, the man who would investigate President Trump.[45] This happened without anyone in the media, or even amongst the Republicans on Capitol Hill, making the obvious observation: how on earth can a man who tried out for one of the most important jobs under the president, but who failed to make the grade, possibly impartially investigate the man in front of whom he so abjectly failed? It would be akin to interviewing with a CEO for one of the C-suite positions in his company and utterly failing, only to be made district attorney immediately thereafter and handed the job of investigating that CEO for corruption. No worse conflict of interest is imaginable. But for Obama and his accomplices, desperate times called for desperate measures, and with a complicit media and a supine GOP, they figured no one would stop them.

In the two years that followed, Mueller tried everything to get dirt on Trump, and in doing so destroyed several people's lives. Paul Manafort may not be a salubrious character, but incarcerating people for mortgage fraud was not Mueller's mandate.[46] Similarly, it was not Mueller's mandate to harass General Mike Flynn—an American patriot who had served his nation with distinction for decades only to lose his home and have the freedom of his family threatened after Mueller charged him with a process crime any American could fall foul of and which had nothing to do with any "collusion."[47]

Remarkably, despite the tens of millions of dollars spent, the inordinate powers vested in a special counsel, the two-thousand eight hundred subpoenas, five hundred search warrants, five hundred witnesses interviewed by forty agents, Mueller couldn't find one piece of evidence linking any American on the Trump campaign to the

Russian government as a conspirator.[48] So what did he do after two years of trying to take down the duly elected president of the United States? In a disgraceful display that epitomizes Team Obama's attitude to rule of law, Mueller upended American jurisprudence on his last day on the job.

In a truly peculiar press conference—only matched in its perversion of our national principles by the one his friend James Comey had given during the presidential campaign season that exonerated Hillary Clinton despite her committing at least one hundred eight felonies by his own count[49]—Robert Mueller actually granted more rights to foreign intelligence agents than he did to the president of the United States. With reference to those Russian military intelligence officers he had charged with attempting to subvert the 2016 presidential election, Robert Mueller stated:

> These indictments contain allegations. And we are not commenting on the guilt or innocence of any specific defendant. Every defendant is presumed innocent unless and until proven guilty in court.[50]

But just a few seconds later, with regard to an American citizen, who doesn't work for Russian intelligence and who happens to be the president of the United States, he said:

> [I]f we had had confidence that the president clearly did not commit a crime, we would have said so. We did not, however, make a determination as to whether the president did commit a crime.[51]

Never in the history of our country has a prosecutor been charged with proving whether an American did not commit a crime. In fact, it is in direct contravention of both Department of Justice regulations, as well as the rules of the American Bar Association, for any prosecutor at any level to ever comment on the guilt or innocence of a person who stands uncharged of any crime. Sean Davis of the *Federalist* had the very best analysis of Mueller's betrayal of our legal system written within hours of his outrageous remarks.[52] First he quoted Department of Justice rules:

> As a series of cases makes clear, there is ordinarily "no legitimate governmental interest served" by the government's public allegation of wrongdoing by an uncharged party, and this is true "regardless of what criminal charges may... b[e] contemplated by the Assistant United States Attorney against the [third-party] for the future,"

followed by the American Bar Association's Rules of Professional Conduct:

> "The prosecutor in a criminal case shall... refrain from making extrajudicial comments that have a substantial likelihood of heightening public condemnation of the accused."[53]

It is impossible that Mueller was not aware of either of these rules, since they stem from the foundational principles of British and American law: a person is innocent until proven otherwise, and the burden of proof lies on government prosecutors, not on the accused.

But this is the measure of the political opponents we face today. We are confronted by a "Resistance" that is opposed to the American Constitution and the traditional rules of law. And that "resistance" has risen to the highest levels of our government. Be it a former president raised in Muslim Indonesia[54] and on the knees of Communists in Hawaii,[55] who became a disciple of the radical Saul Alinsky[56] and a member of the corrupt Chicago Democrat political machine;[57] or a former Communist sympathizer who ended up as director of the CIA;[58] or another as director of the FBI (James Comey);[59] or a former first lady who interned for Communist lawyers in California[60] and wrote her college thesis on Alinsky's rules for subverting a democratic republic,[61] these are the leaders of a Left that wishes to destroy all that is not theirs and rebuild what remains in their own godless image.

But they never counted on Donald Trump.

Some argue that great men are born great. Others that greatness is thrust upon normal men by circumstance, and they must rise to the challenge. In truth, both things obtain at once. Donald Trump is unique. I knew this within minutes of our first meeting in his office in Trump Tower in the summer of 2015. And it became more and more apparent as I came to advise him before his victory and then work for him as his strategist in the White House. At the same time you cannot understand how he became president and the dangers we still face today if you fail to understand what about the years before 2016 made his presidency possible, and how it was that the "forgotten men and women" of America, the "deplorables," were able to rally round and elect a complete and utter outsider, a non-politician, to the presidency of the United States. If we are truly to save our Republic, then we must guarantee another four years of that outsider's tenure in the White House, and that can only be done by understanding how the "elite" betrayed working-class America and how the billionaire from Queens realized that and decided that something had to be done to Make America Great Again.

CHAPTER TWO

THE POLITICAL ELITE'S BIPARTISAN BETRAYAL OF AMERICA

T he ascendency of a total political outsider to the highest position in the land represents a grave threat to the vested interests of the establishment elite on both sides of the political aisle, left and right.

The fact that Donald Trump defeated the Left's anointed candidate, Hillary Clinton, and at the same time vanquished a field of sixteen Republican candidates who themselves were mostly representatives of the establishment class, representing a largely liberal, bipartisan consensus, is remarkable. Add onto this that as a self-made billionaire Donald Trump owes nothing to the political donor class. No president in our lifetime—not even Ronald Reagan—has been more independent, less influenced, or controlled by the political establishment that believes it knows best and should make all the key decisions for the American people.

It was the arrogance—and, frankly, the ignorance—of the American political establishment that sparked the populist revolution that elected President Trump. That establishment was finally being held to account for its massive failures and its betrayal of the American people and our national interests for decades. Here we need not fancy political science theories or polling data on the evolution of political attitudes across the nation. Instead I will share with you the story of one young man, who, though he is no supporter of the president's, through his life and through the vicissitudes his family have had to endure, perfectly illustrates our betrayal by the establishment and why the outcome of election day, November 8, 2016, was even possible.

His background was as difficult as one can imagine. His grandmother once doused his grandfather in gasoline and set him alight. His mother was a drug addict. And his father would always be a stranger. Yet he would become a U.S. Marine and his autobiography would become a national phenomenon.

Of course I am talking about J. D. Vance, the author of the best-selling *Hillbilly Elegy*.[1]

I don't read biographies, auto- or otherwise. I only read non-fiction works of a historical or strategic nature that have a broad scope beyond one person. Oh, and the humor of the late Terry Prachett and Harry Harrison for light relief.

I can't stand the idea of investing tens of hours of my life in reading a three- or four-hundred-page doorstop about one person, with details about what they had for breakfast on February 20, 1962, or what tie they picked for their meeting with Khrushchev. But something drew me to J. D. Vance's story.

First, my wife praised it highly. And she is very choosey. *Very*. Second, it was short.

I love reading, but for some reason, I know not what, I am a very slow reader. *Very*. But I managed to plow through the whole of *Hillbilly Elegy* in one Thanksgiving weekend. This was in part because it is well written. By that I do not mean it is a work of fine literature, a book that will be talked about alongside Shakespeare and Orwell. But it is eminently "readable." Whenever I write, I strive to make each work as accessible to as many people as possible. Having spent twenty years as a professor in Europe and the United States, I still enjoy reading relevant scholarly texts in fields I care about, even if only a handful of other people will ever read them, but long ago I concluded that, for the most part, reading should be of as broad a utility as possible, even fiction.

If you write, you should write about the truth, whether it's about where al Qaeda really came from and what it will take to destroy the culture of jihadism, or a novel, a work of fiction that illuminates eternal truths about humanity, our loves, our travails, or our great victories in the face of overwhelming odds. And since in the age of Twitter, Instagram, YouTube, video streaming, and binge-watching, so very few people take the time to read books at all, I feel that it is incumbent upon the author to dismantle the artificial barriers of style and form when necessary, so that as many people as possible can access and consume what they have to tell us. Anyway, that's my philosophy as an author, and it is very clear that Mr. Vance has a similar one.

If you've never read Vance's book, right about now you're saying to yourself: "Why is Gorka including in his book on the cultural civil war gripping America, a chapter on some self-professed hillbilly made good?" Bear with me.

Donald Trump defeated all comers to win the greatest contest in his life in large part because he connected with so-called "flyover" America, and with all types of Americans, including me, despite my initial reservations. Remember, I was born in London. My parents might have been refugees from Central Europe, but I went through the British education system with all it had to offer during the glorious years under Prime Minister Margaret Thatcher. I had thirteen years with the Benedictines at a private school, studying Shakespeare, the royal history of the British Empire, reciting Latin declensions, joining the debating society, playing cricket and rugby, developing a stiff upper lip, and then heading off to London University to read philosophy and theology. As a result, when I received the phone call to come meet the reality TV show star from Queens to help him prepare on national security issues for the Republican debate, it was not the call I was expecting. Nor did I expect to "connect" with a man who clearly was very different in style and manner to what I had grown accustomed to in England. But I did.

Not only did I connect with the brash billionaire businessman, but once I came to work for him in the White House, I would get to see first hand the preternatural way he connects with people of all backgrounds—especially people who were life-long, working-class Democrat voters, such as the salt of the earth "forgotten men" and women of Pennsylvania or Michigan or Wisconsin.

Take a moment. Wrack your brains. Just try and think of another person today who can, on the one hand, so empathetically connect with a legal immigrant from Europe, classically schooled, who taught strategy to the military for a living, while on the other hand expressing the thoughts, hopes, and desires of an unemployed steel worker from the "Steel Valley" of Ohio. See what I mean? That is so very, very rare an ability. Ronald Reagan could do it. But Jeb Bush certainly couldn't, nor could Ted Cruz or John Kasich. And Hillary Clinton never would, no matter how hard she tried.

So how did he do it? How did the billionaire win over the heart of real America against the desires and expectations of the establishment and the so-called "coastal elite"? Here I must turn back to Mr. Vance's story, because *Hillbilly Elegy* is the clearest expression of what the Left's war on America's soul did to our nation.

Even if you have read the book, indulge me. Allow me to summarize, and more importantly, reframe Vance's story—which was written before we chose Donald Trump to lead our nation—so as to highlight how this moving odyssey of one young American man can help us understand why in fact Donald Trump did win and why he remains such a threat to the liberal establishment and the radical Left. For J. D. Vance may not be a historian or a social scientist or have a Ph.D. in political science, but if you step back and take the tale of a child born into the grinding hardship of a broken home mired within an environment of drugs and unemployment, we will better understand what actually happened on November 8, 2016. We will understand why Donald Trump was in fact the only man who could help those who love our Republic to claw back our nation from those who had misappropriated it for their own ends.

Reading J. D. Vance's story helps us to understand what harm the liberal establishment and a radicalized Left did to America, how they were largely held unaccountable until the election of 2016, and just how high the stakes are if President Trump is not re-elected and we really lose the cultural civil war. J. D Vance's story may be only one man's story, but in many ways it is America's story—or at least a story of the heartland. As Vance says, "I am a hill person. So is much of America's white working class. And we hill people aren't doing very well."[2]

Hillbilly culture is different. And it's not just about people with missing teeth who like banjo music. The hillbilly way follows a code of unwritten rules which revolve around the concept of honor.

J. D. Vance was born into what he calls "hillbilly royalty." In a world where violence was only a careless insult away—his grandmother was never without her .44 magnum revolver—his extended clan's history was replete with stories of "white hats" and "black hats," and his relatives and ancestors were always on the worthy side, the side that was serving something beyond parochial self-interest, be it the family, the nation, or God.

J. D.'s clan was the Blanton clan of Kentucky. More specifically, the Blantons of Jackson, Breathitt County, or as the locals refer to it, "Bloody Breathitt," an indication of how its inhabitants dealt with the malefactors in their midst, this being the hillbilly justice of the tough Appalachian people.

But despite the pride this Blanton scion felt—and still feels today—for the community of his birth, Vance realizes that his home has suffered a traumatic social collapse. As *Hillbilly Elegy* opens, Vance tells of a recent trip back to Jackson, and the sorry sight he witnesses: "decrepit shacks rotting away, stray dogs begging for food, and old furniture strewn on the lawns."[3] With close to a third of Jackson's population living below the poverty line, and that proportion rising to almost half among minors, with local education in such catastrophic shape that the state of Kentucky had to take over the county's schools, there must be an explanation for this collapse, a collapse that is linked to American politics and a culture war.

J. D.'s pride is indelibly mixed with sadness, sadness for a part of America that has lost its way. Badly. But why had this all occurred? It is easy to point at the epidemic of prescription drug abuse but that's not an explanation. That is just a proximate cause. Any American, in any city or town, can become an addict. From the ritziest parts of Manhattan to the most impoverished areas of the rustbelt. So why Jackson? How could the spirit of what is arguably one of the toughest communities in America, of a people who for centuries worked with their hands and their backs, surviving in the very toughest of conditions without the luxuries most Americans take very much for granted, be so badly broken? Why would these life-long fighters surrender to the slow suicide of drug abuse, prescription or otherwise, and lose the will to function as before? This search for an answer is clearly the motivation for Vance's writing *Hillbilly Elegy*, wherein he uses his own life and personal transformation to help find out what really has happened to the heart of America. In doing so he provides an inestimable service to others who want to understand why, for the first time since the signing of the Declaration of Independence, America chose a complete political outsider to be our president. This is why there is a direct line from the hills of Tennessee to today's White House. President Trump's election is a reaction against the Left's all-out assault on all that is good and true in America, an assault seen perhaps most clearly in the impact the Left's culture war has had on middle America—the patriotic, working-class Americans which the Left regards as both deplorable and dispensable.

I am an American by choice. My perspective on our nation is that of the former outsider. My being American was a conscious and very serious choice, not a function of an accident of birth. And as such, for me being an American is an attitude, a state of mind. It has nothing to do with your appearance, your accent, your job, the color of your skin, or how much you earn. My appreciation of the egalitarian nature of America is probably amplified by my experiencing exactly the opposite for the first twenty-three years of my life, growing up in the class-ridden and incredibly stratified social system of the United Kingdom. In England, your future could turn on something as simple as how you pronounce the words "all right." In the United States, you can rise to the highest office in the land even if you were raised by a single mother, the son of an African dead-beat father, and spent part of your childhood in Indonesia with an Indonesian stepfather, as Barack Obama did. (And yet his political party continues to proclaim that America is a land full of racism and oppression.)

As such, I caution anyone who would preemptively draw the conclusion that a socio-economic, cultural, and political analysis of Appalachia is too tight an aperture through which to draw larger, more strategic conclusions about what has happened to America over recent years. Especially if you consider the demographic flows that knit this country together and the patterns of movement in what is, perhaps, the most internally mobile of populations anywhere in the world.

Vance describes how this mobility, the search for work and for better pay, shaped the culture he was born into and how it resulted in hillbilly sensibilities spreading far beyond the hills where they were formed over the centuries. How the so-called "Hillbilly Highway" phenomenon witnessed millions of the Americans who shared his special culture travel north in search of jobs. How after World War II, almost 15 percent of rural Kentuckians left the state as part of a true exodus, so that by 1960 when the total population of Ohio stood at ten million souls, a million of them had moved there from the Appalachian communities of Kentucky, Tennessee, or Virginia. This is why the story of the Blanton Clan into which J. D. Vance was born, is not just the story of one corner of America. It is as American as any other community's story about trying to live the "American Dream."

It is thanks to this internal migration, a pattern we have seen furrowed into the soil of our nation again and again, that Vance was born in 1984 in the town of Middletown, Ohio, where his grandparents had moved two generations earlier in search of gainful employment in what would become the biggest local employer, the American Rolling Mill Company, known as the "Armco" steel mill. This is where we must stake our first marker as we endeavor to explain "What did the Left do to America?" and "Why Trump?"

In the mid-1980s, Middletown was an exemplar of America at work, of the postwar values that turned the United States into the richest and most powerful nation the world had ever seen. People had come to Middletown for work, and they found it. They were paid a decent wage, large enough to raise a family on comfortably, and for many it was the first time they had money to spend. No longer were their lives defined by subsistence, working the land just to stay alive. They now worked for Armco or another major local concern. They could pay their bills with ease, were contributing to pension plans, and then had money left over. This disposable income would become a driver for the local economy, as a shopping center was established, restaurants were opened, and eventually even two malls were built.

In much of the upper Midwest, the story was the same. During World War II America had become a manufacturing powerhouse, and after the war, the bomber plants and tank factories gave way to Ford and GE plants that employed patriotic returning soldiers. We became the largest producer of manufactured products for the world. This meant jobs, it meant wealth creation, and it meant prosperity for those in Appalachia who were prepared to move to these factories and build new lives for themselves, including J. D. Vance's grandparents.

Yet today, the town they chose, Middletown, is an eviscerated shell of its former self. The once thriving community, with its manufacturing firms and abundance of small businesses has become a desolate place where jobs are few and low paying, and much of the town has become derelict.

Why? How did a thriving town become what Vance describes as "a relic of American industrial glory"? How did its Main Street become "the place you avoid after dark"? This level of degradation and decline is unnatural unless a community physically leaves. But Middletown is no ghost town. Many of those who traveled the "Hill-billy Highway," or whose ancestors made the journey, are still there. But many of them are now unemployed and on welfare. Some are drug addicts and essentially unemployable. We are wrong to think of poverty as something located primarily in the black ghettos of the inner cities. As one scholar notes: "Between 1970 and 2000 the percentage of white children living in high poverty neighborhoods increased from 25 percent to 40 percent."[4] Vance cites data from a 2011 Brookings Institution study showing that "compared to 2000, residents of extreme-poverty neighborhoods in 2005–9 were more likely to be white, native-born, high school or college graduates, homeowners, and not receiving public assistance."[5] These Americans would become the "forgotten men and women" so important to the eventual presidential campaign of Donald J. Trump. Such a radical change in the health of a community never happens in isolation, or by accident. There has to be a cause, and Donald Trump is a response to that cause. What is that cause? In short, it is the liberal culture war against middle America. Part of the culture war is the globalist economic war against its interests.

The changes in postwar America, the components of its economic progress, when millions of rural Americans moved north to follow the boom in industrial and manufacturing jobs, were the epitome of the American dream. Vance's grandparents moved to find jobs with Armco. Armco would become the beating heart of Middletown. As long as it could sell its steel and manufacture what American carmakers and power-generating companies around the world needed, this part of Ohio would be a magnet for workers and an engine for prosperity. But something happened along the way that seemed to end the American Dream for millions of Americans.

By the end of the 1980s Armco was in trouble, losing out to foreign competition, and it was forced to partner with the Japanese firm Kawasaki Steel. In the decades that followed, the new firm, AK Steel, would move its headquarters to Pittsburgh, then struggle with enormous debt, only to move back to Middletown. Later investing hugely in a new plant in Rockport, Indiana, AK Steel struggled again with serious management problems and safety concerns. There were ten workplace deaths in less than five years.

One such story, concerning just one town and one American company, should have been an outlier in a nation that had become the most powerful and economically healthy nation after World War II. But Middletown's story became the story of America's manufacturing and industrial heartland. Companies were run down or shut down, acquired for pennies on the dollar by asset strippers. Jobs were outsourced and millions of Americans were left unemployed. Entire communities faced economic decline, neighborhoods deteriorated, social bonds frayed, and into this environment of soul-crushing despair came an influx of drugs that made captives of hopeless people. And none of this was an accident. All of it was the result of economic decisions made by the political and economic establishment.

Growth and prosperity had been something that Americans previously considered natural. In J. D. Vance's words:

> [Y]our dad (or grandpa) was a man with a respected job. It never occurred to me that Armco wouldn't be around forever, funding scholarships, building parks, and throwing free concerts.[6]

Vance goes on to note that his generation, like every previous American generation, believed that they would do better than their parents.

> [F]ew of my friends had ambitions to work there [at Armco]. As small children, we had the same dreams that other kids did; we wanted to be astronauts or football

players or action heroes.... By the sixth grade, we wanted
to be veterinarians or doctors or preachers or businessmen.
But not steelworkers.... We never considered that we'd be
lucky to land a job at Armco; we took Armco for granted.[7]

The reason that the people of Appalachia had upped sticks and
moved far from home for a better life may have been remembered by
their children and grandchildren, but that reality was never deemed
fragile or potentially transitory. In any case, hillbillies are the toughest of the tough. If the conditions in "Bloody Breathitt" couldn't break
these Americans, nothing could. In the hardest of times they would
survive, as the family, as the clan closed together to protect its own.
They may not have had much social capital or savings in the bank,
but they had each other, and they had their own hillbilly honor code
to provide predictability and justice.

In J. D. Vance's case, the code was passed down by his grandparents who taught the rules of hill country comportment, whereby a
careless insult could lead to violence in the blink of an eye. Vance
received his first bloody nose at the ripe old age of six, in the classic
scenario of another child insulting J. D.'s mother, which led to fisti-
cuffs. The rules were simple. A man's honor was sacrosanct. It was
inextricably linked to the sense of his dignity within the community.
Any surrender to forces that led to his disgrace would mean his friends
and family would see him as less of a man, as someone who didn't
deserve respect. And this code applied to women as much as men,
with Vance's grandmother having the high reputation she had within
the community because of stories that she had once killed a man who
dishonored one of her relatives.

This is not to say that these communities were typified by capricious or indiscriminate violence. No, hillbilly communities were the very opposite of an amoral, anarchic society. The honor code of the hills had a foundation, a point of reference that provided the filter through which others could be judged consistently. That filter was faith, the Christian faith that Vance described as providing the "center of our lives." There was a greater yardstick for justice, one that existed outside of the family and the clan. You always did what was right, but "rightness" was not amorphous or subjective; the moral compass was in the Bible for all to read and internalize.

So even the Appalachian transplants to Ohio should have been insulated from the buffeting world around them by their own rules for survival and the surety the Good Book provides. But no. In fact their fate became an indicator of a spreading rot within American society, within the soul of a nation that had prided itself from its inception on the "rugged individualism" of its founders, on the spirit of adventure and iconoclastic self-realization that Tocqueville described so evocatively in his seminal text *On Democracy*. But this sickness had been planted and encouraged by those Americans who do not believe in the eternal truths upon which our nation had been built.

In the life of J. D. Vance, this cultural breakdown was expressed at the micro level by the tailspin his mother spiraled into when he was but a child. An intelligent woman, a trained health worker, she nevertheless found it impossible to deal with the stress of trying to maintain a middle-class life. She succumbed to alcohol abuse, then prescription narcotics, and finally the addiction of hard drugs, which culminated in a wrenching episode Vance describes, in which he saw his mother, out of control, bloodied, and screaming in the front yard, before being placed in the back of a patrol car, only to be eventually admitted to an addiction treatment facility. This left a thirteen-year-old J. D. to fend for himself with the help of his seventeen-year-old sister who was still in high school. In the following months, as they would try to survive in between the visits to see their mother in rehab, he and his sister would be introduced to what the author calls "the underworld of American addiction," to a world where more and more Americans "used drugs to escape the stress of paying bills," bills they couldn't pay because the America they believed in was being deliberately dismantled.

This is where we must stop for a moment and step back from *Hillbilly Elegy* to ask the macro question. How did Vance's mother arrive at the point where taking drugs was even an option, an alternative to paying your bills? Not paying what you owed would have been deemed dishonest, dishonorable by her community's code just a few years prior. How did her story become the story of so many Americans that today more than 70,000 of our fellow citizens die of drug overdoses each year, more than the total number of lives lost in combat during the entirety of the Vietnam War? Such a massive cultural shift never happens in a vacuum, it never happens just by accident. For an answer to this question, which is crucial for us to grapple with if we are to understand how a complete outsider like Donald J. Trump became our president, we need to turn to his former chief strategist, Stephen K. Bannon.

Steve Bannon is an incredibly misunderstood public figure, in part because in the past he has deliberately cultivated a persona to confuse and frustrate his rivals in the media and politics. Variously described as the "Darth Vader of the Right" and "Trump's puppet master," he is neither. In fact, the misrepresentations of my old boss are in part malicious, but in part a function of how unique a path he has trodden.

His life trajectory does not fit into any established and easily comprehended category or taxonomy that a lazy observer may want to force upon him. Born into a Southern, working-class, Irish Catholic family from Richmond, Virginia, Bannon served as an officer in the U.S. Navy, with the Fleet and at the Pentagon, then attended Harvard Business School, ending up as a very successful mergers and acquisitions expert at Goldman Sachs. Later he was a film producer, and eventually a cultural warrior, friend, and business partner of none other than Andrew Breitbart. But most important of all, he is the man who, six weeks prior to the presidential election of 2016, took candidate Trump from a 16-point deficit behind Hillary Clinton, in the middle of the explosive release of the Billy Bush tapes, to a stunning electoral victory. He, more than anyone else I know, can put the millions of stories like J. D. Vance's, into the correct strategic and political context and explain how the "forgotten men and women" were the most important reason for Donald Trump's success.

In an interview with Lou Dobb's of the FOX Business Network, after leaving the White House, Bannon put the suffering of those who built America into strategic context, when he said:

> [H]e's president of the United States because of the rejection of working-class people, middle-class people, about managed decline of our country at the hands of people like Hillary Clinton. *The Clinton Global Initiative*, the whole Clinton apparatus, these globalists and elitists were very

comfortable with the managed decline, particularly *vis-à-vis* the rise of China.

And Donald Trump confronted them, particularly in the upper Midwest. This is the reason why he won states like Ohio, Pennsylvania, Michigan, and Wisconsin. People understand, like J. D. Vance, the great sociologist who wrote the book *Hillbilly Elegy*, the factories went to China, the jobs went to China, and the opioids came in.[8]

And then again within a long interview with Charlie Rose, Bannon unpacked how all of the above was now transmogrified into a platform of "economic nationalism," the philosophy that undergirds the *Make America Great Again* mantra that elevated a populist New York billionaire with no political experience to the White House. While Trump's economic nationalism was at odds with the liberal bipartisan consensus in Washington, it is well-rooted in American history:

America is built on our citizens. Look at the nineteenth century, what we called the American system, from Hamilton to Polk to Henry Clay to Lincoln to the Roosevelts. A system of protection of our manufacturing, a financial system that lends to manufacturers, and the control of our borders. Economic nationalism is what this country was built on. The American system, we're going back to that. We look after our own, we look after our citizens, we look after our manufacturing base, and guess what? This country's gonna be greater, more united, more powerful than it's ever been. And it's not—this is not astrophysics. And by the way, that's for every nationality, every race, every religion, every sexual preference. As long as you're a citizen of our country, as long as you're an American citizen, you're part of this populist, economic nationalist movement.[9]

It was this "American Way" which made the prosperity that J. D. Vance's clan had participated in and profited from possible, that had made us the most powerful and the freest nation in world history. And it was this way of life that the radical Left has systematically dismantled in recent generations with the acquiescence of the political establishment.

And finally in a public debate with one of the pillars of that establishment, David Frum, Steve explained how Donald Trump was in fact the nation's reaction to this "managed decline" piloted by the elite, the antidote to a philosophy of self-loathing which saw America as the problem and not as the greatest experiment in human self-governance:

If you've owned assets, intellectual property, stocks, real estate, a hedge fund, name it, in the last ten years, you had the greatest run in history. For everybody else, a disaster. Fifty percent of American families can't put their hands on $400 of cash. It wasn't Donald Trump, it wasn't the populists [that caused that]. The populist movement, the nationalist movement, it's not a cause of that, it's a product of that. Donald Trump's presidency is not a cause of that, it's a product of that.[10]

This is the macro context into which Donald Trump stepped as the presidential candidate the establishment deemed laughable. But to the tens of millions of Americans who had been forgotten—who had been thrown to the wind by a political class that spent decades making decisions that systematically undermined the culture of working- and middle-class Americans and exported their livelihoods overseas—Trump was the one last hope. That group included J. D. Vance, and this is where we return to his story.

In *Hillbilly Elegy*, J. D. Vance tells how—needing money and desiring a sense of independence—he ended up working as a cashier at the local grocery store. It was the perfect perch from which the bright young teenager could observe and analyze the changes in his community, how a once proud people often became welfare scammers, gaming the system instead of doing an honest day's work. He tells of people who would buy soda in bulk with their government food stamps, sell the bottles for cash on the street corner, and then use the money to buy cigarettes and alcohol. He mentions welfare recipients who spent their days talking on their new cell phones (which Vance himself couldn't afford) and his drug addicted neighbor who ate better on food stamps than Vance and his sister did on his pay check. The government, in short, subsidized dependency, rewarded bad behavior, and effectively discouraged working at a low wage job. (This was why the Obama administration used to brag about its expanding food stamp rolls.)[11]

From his autobiography, it is clear that this is the moment when a teenage hillbilly had an epiphany and began to understand that his grandparents' devotion to Democrat politics and "the party of the working man" wasn't paying the dividends promised for so long to the American working class and middle class. Taxing the working man and woman to help those who needed help wasn't meant to provide booze and drugs to the unemployed; it wasn't meant to subsidize drug addicts like Vance's neighbor Patti, who one day called her landlord to tell him to fix her leaky roof. On his arrival, what did the landlord find? Patti half naked and passed out on prescription painkillers as water dripped through the ceiling from the bath she had left running upstairs. This economic, cultural, and social decline was the hellish and transformative journey that too many Americans made as the world around them changed in ways that they had no control over, as the sheltered elite which Bannon described created the conditions that not even the hardened culture of the hillbilly clan could overcome. In one passage, Vance summarizes it so well:

> When the factories shut their doors, the people left behind were trapped in towns and cities that could no longer support such a large population with high-quality work. Those who could—generally the well educated, wealthy, or well connected—left, leaving behind communities of poor people. These remaining folks were the "truly disadvantaged"—unable to find good jobs on their own and surrounded by communities that offered little in the way of connections or social support.[12]

These are the people that Hillary Clinton so cynically called the "basket of deplorables" during the election campaign, a move that she must regret to this day, given that these communities became the key to Donald Trump's victory, the name "Deplorable" eventually being used as a moniker of pride by the future president's staunchest supporters. It would be millions of Americans like the author of *Hillbilly Elegy* who would see a ray of hope in the candidacy of Donald Trump.

America's promise of economic opportunity had been broken. Who better to restore it than a patriotic, populist businessman who spoke the language of working people and understood their problems? The policymaking class, which was meant to consist of "citizen politicians" in the spirit of our Founding Fathers, had devolved into a "swamp" of professional politicians, many of whom spent decades in office, inexplicably ending up as multi-millionaires on a government wage, while dismissing the "deplorables" as losers within the liberal economic system that both parties promoted.

Let us not forget the truly historic nature of what happened on November 8, 2016. All forty-four of America's previous presidents, from George Washington to Barack Obama, had been established politicians or senior military officers before becoming commander in chief. Every single one had been either a governor, a senator, a congressman, or a general. Not Donald Trump.

How did this happen? How did a brusque real-estate magnate from Queens who had a reality TV show become our forty-fifth president? The election of Donald Trump was only possible because of a bipartisan betrayal of middle America. The radical Left set the agenda, the Democrat party promoted it, and the Republican party largely accepted it immediately or in due course. Donald Trump was the sole alternative to managed American decline that rewarded the establishment at the expense of working- and middle-class American citizens. How did the Left plan to subvert America, and who were the main perpetrators? Read on, dear friend, read on.

CHAPTER THREE

THE PLOTTERS— AND THEIR PLAN—TO DESTROY AMERICA

O n a crisp, clear November night in Berlin thirty years ago, we won the Cold War. Or did we?

That war had begun forty-one years earlier in the same city when America's World War II ally, the Soviet Union, decided to blockade Allied access to the sectors of Berlin that were under Western control after 1945. Stalin had control of all of East Germany, but of only one of the four sectors into which the former Reich capital had been divided after the collapse of Hitler's regime. Stalin wanted it all, and because Berlin was deep within East Germany, he assumed that using his Red Army to isolate the Western sectors held by France, Britain, and the United States would be easy. On April 1, 1948, Soviet

troops blocked the roads in occupied Berlin and barred all civilian
and military traffic that wasn't authorized by Moscow.

Stalin's plan eventually backfired as the Allies refused to relin-
quish the innocent people in their sectors to Stalin's Communist forces
and instead initiated the greatest airlift resupply in history. To break
the Berlin Blockade, which lasted from June 1948 until May 1949,
when Stalin reopened the land routes, the Allies flew 2,326,406 tons
into an effectively besieged West Berlin,[1] landing a plane every thirty
seconds.[2] Stalin's failed aggression against West Berlin was the tangible start of the Cold War.

For the next forty-one years the Communist East was pitted
against the Capitalist West in an arms race, as well as dozens of local
wars and proxy conflicts in which Soviet-aligned forces fought
America-aligned forces. The competition was fierce and more than
once almost precipitated disaster, most obviously in October 1962
during the Cuban Missile Crisis. The root cause of all this—the
ideological incompatibility of communism with the free societies of
the West—could have only one of four outcomes: an endless Cold
War that turned occasionally hot on the global periphery; a world
war where both sides abstained from resorting to nuclear weapons,
and one side militarily defeated the other; an armed conflict in
which nuclear missiles were used and neither side could be said to
have won; or the scenario which came to pass: that the inhuman,
totalitarian Communist system founded on the ideas of Karl Marx
collapsed in on itself. The enslaved people of the Soviet Union and
the Eastern Bloc finally tore down the walls of tyranny brick by
brick—or in the case of Berlin, concrete slab by concrete slab on
November 9, 1989.

Just a year and a half earlier, President Ronald Reagan had stood at the Berlin Wall, the most powerful symbol of a world divided, separated by those who had freedom and those who lived in Communist slave states, and demanded of the Soviet premier, Mikhail Gorbachev, "Tear down this wall!"[3] Gorbachev never tore down the Berlin Wall, but those who had been captive behind it for decades were inspired and their morale strengthened by Reagan's words, and soon enough their time would come.

The most liberal of Soviet satellite regimes, the Communist government of Hungary would lead the way. Seeing the writing on the wall, finally acknowledging the truth that communism was a political and economic failure that could not be maintained, the government in Budapest took the shocking step of opening Hungary's border with Austria, allowing Hungarians to travel to freedom and the West. In May 1989, the Communist government ordered border guards to remove sections of barbed wire along the border. In June, the foreign ministers of Communist Hungary and the free Republic of Austria together ceremonially cut the barbed wire that was part of the "Iron Curtain."

East Germany was—save perhaps Albania and Romania—the most oppressive of the Communist Warsaw Pact nations. Positioned as it was next door to the free Federal Republic of West Germany, which had become an incredibly successful country and an economic powerhouse, the East German regime greatly feared for the future of its Communist "paradise" with such a seductive—and free—alternative Germany just across the border. In fact, that is why the Communists had originally built the Berlin Wall in 1961—to divide the city and prevent East Germans from escaping to freedom.

It was this geographic reality that helped in part to make East Germany so repressive, more authoritarian than other Warsaw Pact Communist satrapies like Poland, Czechoslovakia, or Hungary, a true police state held together by a vicious network of the STASI, East Germany's own version of the KGB.

The hardline East German government was shocked when Hungary opened its border to Austria because, while East German citizens weren't free to travel to the West, they could vacation in other Communist countries, Hungary included, and that meant they could now escape to the free world. The Hungarian government announced that it would do nothing to stop them. The Iron Curtain was rent. And so it was that on September 10, 1989, thirty-three years and three days after the Hungarian Revolution that had seen my father liberated from a Communist prison and escape to the West, the Cold War that had threatened the survival of the human race began its end. Twenty-eight years after building the Berlin Wall to keep its citizens trapped inside East Germany, the acolytes of Karl Marx had lost control. If people wanted to escape via Hungary, they could, and they did, crossing into Austria, and then into West Germany to be reunited with family members they might not have seen in three decades or more. Within two months, the Communist system had effectively collapsed, and on that crisp November night the Berlin Wall came down.

The decrepit nature of Communism became clear for all to see. Even those who had fared well by being members of the party elite— who never had to worry about food rationing or the dreaded "2 A.M. knock" on the door if they fell out of favor with the state security apparatus—knew that they could no longer resist popular pressure; their Communist governments and economies were no longer feasible.

With the legitimacy of Karl Marx's ideas demonstrably laughable, economies that were bleeding out, and a West that was more powerful and wealthy than any Leninist pamphlet could ever admit, the usual reliance on brute force was impracticable. By the winter of 1989, the ability to use tanks to suppress the call for freedom—as had been done in Hungary in 1956 and in Czechoslovakia in 1968—or the imposition of martial law, as had been the last desperate move of an ailing regime in Poland in 1981, was simply out of the question, because too many of the people commanding and manning the tanks and the guns had had enough.

And so it was, that after a comical late-night press conference by a misinformed party official who said the East German regime would be changing its laws on citizens who wanted to visit the West, the imprisoned people of East Berlin took to the streets with hand tools and the will to change history. That night, with chisels, hammers, and picks, they went at the wall that had become a symbol of all that is evil about communism. They dismantled and climbed over it to freedom—crossing over to West Berlin. At least one hundred forty fellow Germans had been killed or died at the Berlin Wall over the previous twenty-eight years of Communist oppression.[4] Now the people of East Germany were free.

I was eighteen as I watched world history change before my eyes that night. Sitting in our home in West London, the child of parents who had crossed from East to West and almost been killed as they did so, with a father who had been tortured and imprisoned by a system that he thought would be around long after he died, I watched the incredible images on the news bulletin that dominated all channels that night. The images were unforgettable: triumphant East Germans, released from their captivity, smiling at shocked yet impassive border-guards, climbing a wall that had cost so many lives, with champagne bottles in their hands, crying, smiling, singing as they were met by friends, relatives, and joyous strangers on the other side.

It was a euphoric time. It was a historic time. And it was part of a series of events that changed my life and my parents' lives forever. In its dying days, the Communist regime in Hungary reached out to my father in London—not to torment him, but to try to make amends. They reinstated his Hungarian citizenship and that of my mother, and they expunged the death sentence and warrant on his head for having escaped from political prison during the Hungarian Revolution in 1956. We would eventually all return to visit the land of their birth, where they were reunited with old friends, family members, and former brothers-in-arms. And since I had served in a NATO military, the British Territorial Army, and spoke fluent Hungarian, I would end up with a job offer to work for the first freely elected, post-Communist Conservative government as an official in the Hungarian Ministry of Defense. Soon after that, my parents moved back to Hungary too. (For more details of the amazing journey I was blessed to undertake as a result of the above historic events, see my two previous books, *Defeating Jihad: The Winnable War* and *Why We Fight: Defeating America's Enemies with No Apologies*.)

My parents have since passed away, but they did so back in the country of their birth, laid to rest in the country that they thought they would be exiled from for the rest of their lives. I spent fifteen years in a free, post-Communist Hungary doing my small part to help get the nation of my ancestors back into the community of free nations that comprise Judeo-Christian civilization. You can understand why

I, among many other scholars, was convinced that we, the West, had slain the dragon that was communism, killed the ideology of Marx, Lenin, and Stalin. Scholars as revered as Francis Fukuyama even wrote successful books on how all evil ideologies had been vanquished by the West, and how the future belonged to market democracies. Oh how wrong we all were.

Yes, America and her allies may have defeated the deadly, totalitarian regimes of national socialism and fascism in World War II and communism in the Cold War, but neither ideology is dead. In fact, communism is very, very much alive today. And I am not referring to China, North Korea, or Cuba. Yes, they are all Communist regimes, which have survived the fall of the Berlin Wall and the Soviet Union. What I am talking about is the Communist and socialist threat inside America, a threat that has internalized key elements of fascism to boot. We may have won the Cold War with the Soviet Union and its slave satellites, but thirty years later, the internal threat from those who wish to dismantle our nation from the inside is greater than it has been since the Civil War.

Consider this: today in America, one of the two parties which divide power between themselves is most often represented by a group of freshman congresswomen, the so-called "Squad"—although I prefer "The Four Horsewomen of the Democrat Apocalypse"—made up of Alexandria Ocasio-Cortez, Ilhan Omar, Rashida Tlaib, and Ayanna Pressley.[5]

Two of these women are actually members of the Democratic Socialists of America and were elected to office as such. Together these four—who have within the space of less than six months managed to box the establishment Democrats, including their titular leader,

Nancy Pelosi, into an irrelevant corner—have openly, either individually or as a group, espoused the following extreme stances:

- Demanded the dissolution of the Immigration and Customs Enforcement agency and the Department of Homeland Security
- Advocated open, unsecured borders with Mexico
- Supported taxpayer-funded health insurance for illegal aliens
- Called the Department of Homeland Security's holding facilities for illegal immigrants "concentration camps"
- Denounced Israel as an "evil" nation that has hypnotized the West
- Accused Jewish-American lawmakers of having dual loyalties
- Stated that "brown and black faces" must have "brown and black voices" and that all homosexuals must have one "queer voice," and that none of these voices can dissent from their socialist agenda
- Described the horrendous attacks of September 11, 2001, as "some people did something"
- Refused to denounce the violent acts of Antifa, al Qaeda, and ISIS
- Proposed a gargantuan overhaul of the United States economy under the banner of a "Green New Deal" that would cost $90 trillion dollars to implement and would lead to the banning of gasoline-powered engines and private air travel, as well as the demolition and

reconstruction of any building deemed "environmentally unsound"

And this is just a fraction of the outrageous things that Ocasio-Cortez,
Omar, Tlaib, and Pressley have said since the 2018 elections.

How did we get here? How did these women—with their anti-
Semitic, un-American, socialist views and their extremist identity politics—become the face of the Democrat party? Well it was no accident.

Here we could spiral down a rabbit hole of historic investigation,
but I will be as succinct and as operational as I can be, mindful of the
fact that all you need right now are the most pertinent facts that will
arm you in your political fight to support the Make America Great
Again agenda and help secure the future of our nation.

As before, I owe a debt of gratitude to the late, great Andrew
Breitbart and his autobiography *Righteous Indignation*, chapter six
of which is the most cogent description of how the crazy Leftists plot-
ted—and succeeded—to capture American politics and culture. Please
read Andrew's story for yourself after you have finished with this
book. In the meantime, here is a summary of how the New Left plot-
ted to capture America's soul, and almost totally succeeded before the
outsized outsider from Queens ran for president and defeated them—
at least temporarily.

The fundamentals are clear enough. The New Left in America
can trace its genetic roots back to Jean-Jacques Rosseau, who almost
single-handedly upended centuries of Western philosophical and
theological wisdom.

Instead of believing that man is fallen, fatally flawed, and prone
to selfishness and evil, Rousseau denied the reality of thousands of

years of human history and posited that man was inherently good and that his "goodness" could be maximized if we turned away from the idea of individual rights, liberties, and duties, and instead focused on the communal "will of the people" where the good of the whole would outweigh that of the individual, and we could socially engineer a better society. Rousseau's vision was central to Karl Marx's subsequent development of the collectivist ideology of communism.

Like an ideological scrapbooker, Marx picked and purloined the ideas of others to build his philosophy. He took the ideas of the perfectibility of man and communalism from Rousseau. Marx stole the idea of "historical materialism" from Friedrich Engels. He lifted the idea of inevitable progress (in Marx's vision, to communism) from Hegel and his eponymous "dialectic." Hegel, a profoundly religious man, unlike the rabidly and militantly atheist Marx, saw the history of man as a perpetual progression, a series of qualitative improvements in our collective lot as one new idea (antithesis) reacted against an existing idea (thesis) and resulted in an improved conceptualization (synthesis) that has more truth value than the previous two ideas combined. This progression, so Hegel believed, would increase our enlightenment, until we perceived the ultimate synthesis, the purest version of truth's expression, which is God Himself.

Marx took Hegel's key dynamic and utterly removed God and truth. For Marx the intangible was irrelevant. All that mattered was matter, and so was born his "dialectic materialism," in which the thesis and antithesis were expressions of the inherent conflict within society, the clash between the haves and have-nots, the oppressor and the oppressed, the capitalist and the exploited workers, which would result in a final revolution after which there would be no classes, and the vaunted "means of production," the factories that produced the wealth, would belong to everyone, and we would all live in a just world without any exploitation.

No, seriously, this garbage is what Karl Marx sold with his books *Das Kapital* and *The Communist Manifesto*. And, incredibly, some people believed this rubbish. So much so that they used it as a blueprint to sabotage and subvert multiple nations around the world, starting with Tsarist Russia and stretching all the way to Cuba and China. But then there was a problem. For all their attempts to try and effect a Communist revolution in Western Europe and the United States, Marx's followers failed. And, as Andrew Breitbart points out in his book, America was an especially tough nut for Marx's followers to crack because of how our nation was born. Our Founding Fathers knew full well that man is fallen and tends toward the selfish and the bad. They understood the necessity of having a government with checks and balances and a separation of powers. And they bequeathed us a written constitution founded not on some absurd utopian collectivist vision of society, but built upon the recognition of the unalienable God-given rights we possess, including the rights guaranteed to us by the Bill of Rights. America has had "progressive" presidents and liberal presidents, but it has remained a staunchly unsocialist Republic. Marx's disciples, however, aren't ready to surrender. This is where the influence of a hunchback Italian cripple comes in.

Antonio Francesco Gramsci is the ideational grandfather to all that threatens modern America and our freedoms today, from Alexandria Ocasio-Cortez's Green New Deal to the violence of Antifa. His writings, penned in an Italian prison cell, would be leveraged by the Hungarian Jewish writer and politician, Gyorgy Lukacs, each sharing the conviction that communism had failed in established Western democracies—as opposed to the backward and mostly peasant society of Tsarist Russia—because these societies are too resilient and too developed. For Marxism to flourish in the rest of Europe and America, these "bourgeois" societies must be dismantled piece by piece. From the inside. The New Left took that realization and from it fashioned a political platform that now forms the Democrat Party's articles of belief: from Obamacare's unprecedented intrusion into private healthcare choices to the anti-scientific insanity of transgenderism and beyond. This isn't a random accusation, devoid of context, an accusation floating in space. The path from Gramsci and Lukacs to Alexandria Ocasio-Cortez and Ilhan Omar can be mapped historically, geographically, and institutionally.

Institutionally, the story moves to Germany and a wealthy philosophical playboy named Felix Weil, who used his family's wealth to make a home for these radical ideas under the name, the Institute for Social Research. (Funny how they always find the most innocuous and anodyne labels for their nefarious activities.) You may have heard of the institute by its other name, based upon where it was founded: the Frankfurt School. Here Weil gave a home to Lukacs, as well as to a German philosopher named Max Horkheimer, a man most Americans have never heard of but whose lethal ideas now dominate American colleges.

Horkheimer, like Gramsci and Lukacs, recognized that Marxism would not prevail against established and robust developed societies. The status quo in the West was simply immune to radical ideas of "social justice" and equality enforced by state fiat. So he came up with an otherwise inoffensive-sounding weapon to destroy that status quo: Critical Theory. According to this "theory" which now dominates the social sciences across America and most of the Judeo-Christian world, the current state of affairs must be relentlessly challenged on all fronts. Because power is in the hands of those who do not deserve it, all standing relationships and all dominant concepts must be criticized and dismantled, even language itself, until modern society lies deconstructed, in pieces, and incapable of defending itself from being rebuilt along Marxist lines.

Horkheimer recruited fellow-traveler philosophers who hated the traditions of the West—including Herbert Marcuse, Theodor Adorno, and Erich Fromm. Their names are revered by today's Leftist radicals who have put into action their prescription that the West's Judeo-Christian, democratic, and capitalist institutions must be repeatedly attacked until their collapse, starting with the family and ending with the nation-state itself.

However, as Horkheimer built his team of academic revolutionaries, history intervened. With the rise of Hitler, the future of these avowed Marxists, many of whom were also Jewish, was grim if they stayed in Germany. So where did they go? You guessed it. With the usual open heart and open arms we have shown to those persecuted in their own nations, we Americans welcomed the Frankfurt School's subversives to our shores, more specifically to Princeton, Columbia, Brandeis, and the University of Chicago.

In the years following the war, the proponents of Critical Theory would work their insidious Marxist magic on pillar after pillar of American society, finding their own fellow travelers, starting with journalist Edward R. Murrow, and moving through to other incredibly influential cultural actors such as Dr. Benjamin Spock. Spock adopted their radical ideas, advocated their use in a new way to raise American children, and wrote a revolutionary book titled *The Common Sense Book of Baby and Child Care*, which would go on to sell more than fifty million copies. Marcuse took the "deconstructionist" ideas of his mentor Martin Heidegger and promulgated them across academe until he was recognized as the father of the New Left. (Heidegger's ideas were also central to the ideology of Adolf Hitler and the Third Reich, underlining, again, that Marxism, fascism, and National Socialism have much in common.)

Marcuse's genius was to see that the Marxist expectation of a revolution happening in America was a fantasy. Marx predicted the ineluctable clash with the capitalists and the bourgeois because sooner or later the working class would simply have enough of being "exploited," and the class war would explode by itself. But Marcuse realized that America is a nation uniquely unburdened by a class structure, at least in the way most European nations are defined along incredibly strict stratifications of class distinction, down to how one's class can be identified almost immediately just by one's accent.

In America, the boundless upward mobility afforded by a republic based on the rights of the individual as opposed to the privileges of a special class, are how an autodidact prairie lawyer like Abraham Lincoln could become president, or how Barack Obama, the biracial son of a single mother, could do exactly the same thing. Fomenting a class war was clearly not going to work in a country where even the idea of class distinctions was frowned upon by the majority. Social strife was to be exacerbated so that established societal structures could be dismantled. Marcuse found another dividing line that could be exploited to exacerbate social strife and dismantle societal structures—"victim groups." Who needs a proletariat to build a revolution on, when you can say that women are victimized by men, when you can perpetuate a sense of exploitation by stoking tension between white Americans and non-white Americans, or even between homosexual Americans and their heterosexual neighbors? Andrew Breitbart, as usual, so eloquently expresses this approach when he describes Marcuse's mission "to dismantle American society by using diversity and 'multiculturalism' as crowbars with which to pry the structure apart, piece by piece."[6]

And what would be the best weapon to effect the assault on the structures of society, to maximize the tension between victim and oppressor? Well, quite simply, totalitarianism. But how could you sell totalitarianism to an America coming out of a world war against Hitler and engaged in a cold war with Stalin and heading into the age of love and "flower power"? Easy. In a move that would have astounded even George Orwell, Marcuse instructed his acolytes to sell their totalitarianism as tolerance, "partisan tolerance," which he introduced in an essay he penned in 1965 as a guide for how to shut down debate and silence the critics of Critical Theory. Now bear with me here because this is a real humdinger.

According to Marcuse, classic tolerance has failed our societies. Why? Well because it tolerates all ideas, even those that are "wrong." As a result, tolerance as it has been practiced since the word has had any meaning at all is in fact "repressive tolerance," since it permits the expression of "unjust" views that perpetuate exploitation and oppression. As a result, we must redefine tolerance in such a way that oppression is removed. Meaning that from now on, one need only tolerate that which does not maintain established societal norms of "oppression." Tolerance, to be "real" tolerance from now on must be "partisan tolerance." Did you follow that? This lunacy tracks beautifully with Orwell's novel *1984*, wherein Big Brother states again and again that "war is peace" and "freedom is slavery."

Now before you say: "Enough already! Stop it with the crazy professors!" just consider this: what Marcuse sold his fellow radicals as "partisan tolerance" in 1965 is today's political correctness. Marcuse is why today an observant Jew like Dennis Prager is labeled a bigot and a Nazi on internal Google emails, why conservative speakers are disinvited from speaking on college campuses, where antisemitic initiatives like the Boycott, Divestment, and Sanctions movement against Israel are celebrated, and why anyone who calls a man a man on Twitter can be summarily suspended for "dead-naming" if that man just happens to have declared himself a woman yesterday.

Now you can see how Alexandria Ocasio-Cortez and Ilhan Omar are not fringe accidents but the direct consequence of a long degeneration that began when a Marxist intellectual realized there was no way to take over the countries of the free West except from the inside? Even so, you cannot get from Antonio Gramsci to Alexandria Ocasio-Cortex without mentioning one more person—the person who was, and remains, a muse and a hero to so many radical leftists, and who was in fact the subject of Hillary Clinton's dissertation at Wellesley, Saul Alinsky. To quote Breitbart again:

> [I]f Marcuse was the Jesus of the New Left, then Alinsky was his Saint Paul, proselytizing and dumbing down Marcuse's message, making it practical, and convincing leaders

to make it the official religion of the United States, even if that meant discarding the old secular religion of the United States, the Constitution.

[And his book] *Rules for Radicals* might just as well be entitled *How to Take Over America from the Inside*. It's theory made flesh. Alinksy laid it out step by step, but we were too busy fighting the results to reread his game plan.[7]

(Man, Andrew was good. Please read his book *Righteous Indignation* after you've finished this one.)

Alinsky is the first modern "community organizer." And a Communist too, but a pragmatic one, and a realist who knew from experience what would work and what wouldn't when you faced a much stronger foe. He knew how to co-opt the people you need to co-opt. And he knew how to start the revolution on the inside of the structures you wish to take control of, as opposed to trying to destroy them from the outside.

Andrew provides a superb summary in chapter six of his book on how Alinksy took the abstruse and pretentious ideas of the Frankfurt School and turned them into clear and actionable rules for war, a war with Judeo-Christian civilization informed above all else by the maxim that the ends justify the means. For a blow-by-blow account of who Alinsky was and what he believed, read that chapter in *Righteous Indignation*, or even better read the original *Rules for Radicals*, which is just a small paperback.

But for our purposes here, in order to understand what the Left has become and how Donald Trump remains our only hope to stop the otherwise inexorable forward march of Gramsci's frightful offspring, here are the key elements of Alinsky's strategy to destroy all that is good in America so it can be replaced with a Marxist horror.

As you read them, think about where you see these axioms being deployed today in American politics and what it will take to face up to and defeat them.

- Live by the Rule of Personal Destruction. Treat your adversary as inhuman, deserving zero respect or compassion. Whether it is Sarah Palin, Judge Brett Kavanaugh, or President Donald Trump, identify the targets, immobilize them, make your attack personal, and polarize public opinion about them; demonize them until they are deemed evil.
- The establishment abhors being ridiculed. Use ridicule to make the establishment uneasy and subvert its legitimacy.
- Put pressure on your foe and never let up; always be on the offensive so your enemy can never rest and never regroup.
- Label your opponents hypocrites and pounce mercilessly if they ever fail to live up to their own standards.
- Never go beyond your expertise—but force your enemy outside of his.
- Never rest after a victory. Pile on as your foe is still in shock. Show no pity.
- Your actions are important only insofar as they force your enemies to misstep or overreact. Look at yourself

as a provocateur whose mission is to drive your enemies into making mistakes again and again until their position is untenable.

- Power is measured by how strong your enemy believes you too be. Never let your foe have an accurate measure of your strength. Disinformation and deception are your friends.

These are the rules that have been used against our nation and our values since the 1960s. Because of Alinsky-inspired leftists, we have "identity politics" that pits Americans against each other based upon our skin color, our sex, and even our sexual preferences. The fundamental building block of civilization, the nuclear family, has been gravely weakened, especially in the black community where fatherless homes have become the norm. Thanks to Marcuse's ideas and Alinsky's tactics, many Americans have been brainwashed into believing that killing a viable child in a woman's womb is analogous to birth control. Women have been convinced that they should be like men, and that pursuing demanding careers should be their priority—even at the expense of marriage and motherhood. We have been lulled into thinking recreational drugs aren't so bad for society and that some of them should be legalized. And when it comes to our place in the world, many Americans now believe that America— our power, position, and example—is a problem. Global poverty, war, injustice, and environmental doom are all our fault, they say or imply, and the least we can do is open our borders and allow the rest of the planet to take whatever is left as we slide into an inevitable and necessary decline.

This was the power of the Frankfurt School, and this was our fate, until someone called Donald J. Trump said: "No. America was great, and we can Make America Great Again."

Now the question we have to ask is: can he do it?

CHAPTER FOUR

CAN PRESIDENT TRUMP STOP THE RADICAL LEFT?

O nly a fool would think that the 2016 election was not a historic turning point.

When sixty-three million Americans chose—for the first time since 1776—a non-politician businessman to be president of the United States—they sent a message of just how unsatisfied they were with the political establishment. Nevertheless, this victory of the people over the entrenched coastal centers of political, corporate, and media power was not final in any sense of the word. The media attacks against President Trump have been unrelenting. One Harvard study put some mainstream media coverage (CNN and NBC) at 93 percent negative.[1] The D.C. swamp-dwellers have been equally unrelenting in trying to sabotage President Trump's administration, most obviously by empaneling a deeply biased special prosecutor's team, full of Democrat party donors,[2] to go after the president without any reasonable cause. And unabashed, the Left has doubled down on their objective to subvert the will of the American people with continuing calls for impeachment. Even the relatively sane Nancy Pelosi is on the record saying, "We cannot accept a second term for Donald Trump if we are going to be faithful to our democracy and to the Constitution of the United States."[3] In other words, the leader of the House Democrats believes her party needs to deny democracy and the Constitution in order to save it!

To those of us in the arena—people like myself who have served in the Trump White House and who are on the national stage openly supporting his agenda to Make America Great Again—the fight is a daily one, executed at bayonet distance in the trenches of the mainstream press and social media. It is important, however, for us all to truly understand the extraordinary events we are experiencing, to be able to put it in the right historic and strategic context, to understand not simply why our choice for president was so consequential, but also to see clearly what the Left has done since "the wrong candidate" won, what they are prepared to do to steal back power, and how we can stop them.

To that end I have recruited two of the greatest minds in North America to provide you with the context of the threat to our Republic and predict what the future holds.

One is Professor Victor Davis Hanson, America's preeminent conservative writer, commentator, and strategic thinker. The other is Lord Conrad Black, a remarkably accomplished historian and incredibly successful businessman who has the benefit of having known the president in private life and even negotiated with the master of the "art of the deal."

Let us start with Professor Victor Davis Hanson of the Hoover Institution at Stanford University.

Professor Hanson is a remarkable man. Recognized for decades as a leading classics scholar, he is not a person who sits isolated in his ivory tower; rather, he brings his massive learning to bear on the events we are experiencing in today's world.

A man who grew up on a farm and who has seen what unfettered immigration and collectivist politics have done to the once paradisiacal state of California, Professor Hanson has seen first hand how the liberal elite's intellectual and moral bankruptcy is destroying the American Dream, and understood early on that it would take a total political outsider like Donald Trump to save our nation.

Professor Hanson has written scores of incredibly insightful analyses on "the Trump Effect" for such thoughtful, pro-Trump platforms as American Greatness (www.AmGreatness.com), and this year published a stand-alone treatise titled, *The Case for Trump*.

I have always been impressed with Professor Hanson's work—and never more so than after he publicly stated his support for the president and his agenda, exposing himself to the slings and arrows of 95 percent of his professorial colleagues. That is why I was so delighted when Professor Hanson agreed to grant me an exclusive interview on what the Left has done to our country, why only Donald Trump was the answer, and whether we will win in 2020 and beyond. My first question was whether Professor Hanson would ever have imagined a president of the United States needing to remind Democrat members of Congress—in his State of the Union address—that America would not become a socialist state, that it would not adopt a failed and extreme ideology that cost the lives of a hundred million people in just the last century. Read on![4]

> **VDH:** Well, you know, I heard things when I was younger, in my early teens in the 1960s. That was a pretty turbulent time in American history, there was the SDS [the radical, left-wing Students for a Democratic Society], the Weathermen, and so on, and you would hear things like that, but it was always confined to the fringe. And then growing up on a farm, I'd hear my grandfather talk about there being Socialists during the Depression, [like] Eugene Debs.... But all of these were fringe groups, third-party candidates, or they were agitators. I never saw a phenomenon as we did in 2016, where Bernie Sanders came within a few points of getting the Democratic nomination. So that is new. And then somebody like AOC [Representative Alexandria Ocasio-Cortez] or Representative Ilhan Omar, who are openly Socialist—that's new. It used to be that Bernie Sanders was considered a crack. I think he's been a representative or senator from Vermont for almost 30 years now, since his mid-forties. And it was always, if you went to Vermont, you'd hear them say, "Oh, good old Bernie." He was kind of a nice socialist, but nobody took him seriously.
>
> And then all of a sudden, out of nowhere, in his mid-seventies, we're supposed to consider him now a sober and judicious person? So that's different. We have this young

generation that's poorly educated, one trillion-and-a-half dollars in debt, their demography is very anemic, they're not marrying, they're not buying homes, they're not having children, at an age where most Americans of prior generations did.

I guess this is a long-winded answer, but it's still very disturbing to see socialism mainstreamed like that.

GORKA: Did you ever think, born and bred in the United States, that we would have the federal intelligence community, the federal police, involved in a political spying campaign in 2016 and 2017, which probably will, when we find out the full facts, greatly overshadow Watergate, Professor Hanson?

VDH: No, because it's different than Watergate in the sense that it's not an isolated branch of government, or it's not a rogue group, or it's not a cover-up. It's a systematic weaponization of the hierarchy in the Obama administration, the CIA, the FBI, the DOJ, elements of the State Department, and it follows on the heels of the weaponization, for example, of the IRS, with Lois Lerner going after the Tea Party.

Also, during Watergate, you had an adversarial press, a sort of self-appointed watchdog. We have a fusion now between the Democrat party, the progressive movement, and the media. So, all of a sudden, the media, who used to say they were defenders of civil liberties, now say you cannot investigate the FBI, you cannot endanger the redactions coming out of the CIA, you cannot dare suggest that members of the State Department or DOJ were involved in this. That's new. And that's very scary because freedoms are usually lost when the media joins the government.

Whatever you say about Trump, the Left and the media are hostile to him. But neither Trump nor anyone in the Trump administration that I know of, has said, "Let's go after the left-wing, Soros-funded groups with IRS audits," or, "Let's have the IRS deny them non-profit status," like Lois Lerner did for Obama [with the Tea Party groups]. President Trump's Attorney General William Barr isn't saying, "Let's go after these Associated Press reporters, or James Rosen of Fox, and surveil them the way Obama did." That hasn't happened.

Much less are the people at the FBI or the CIA saying, "You know what, this upcoming election, we have suspicions that the Democratic candidate might be influenced by Iran, or by Mexico, and therefore we're going to surveil them." Whatever happened in 2016, and we still don't know the full extent of it, I don't think there's a parallel unfortunately in American history.

GORKA: Talking to experts who've been investigating these issues for two years now—the John Solomons and the Sara Carters of the world—they say we know between 10 percent and 30 percent of the facts of the "Russiagate" or "Spygate" conspiracies. Based upon what we know already, Professor Hanson, where would this rank in terms of political conspiracies, political scandals in American history? How high does it get on the list of truly insidious plots?

VDH: Well, I'm afraid it's going to be the highest, because those of the past have been confined to one or two individuals as cabinet officers, but this thing could involve corruption from the CIA, which was using its foreign power prerogatives to go after American citizens, and it could include corruption from the FBI, which deliberately led a campaign of distortion and leaking. I've never heard of the FBI director leaking confidential memos, and classified memos, to the press for the express purpose of getting a special counsel, who was then his close friend, appointed to go after his boss, the new president.

And then when you add the distortion of the FISA courts, or you look at using a political candidate's funds to hire a foreign national, Christopher Steele, who then in turn enlisted other foreign nationals to subvert a campaign, as they did with Russian sources, and then you package that whole thing into the context that they are accusing, projection-style, President Trump of doing that—it just never ends.

GORKA: So the Russiagate hoax, the conspiracy, the *Crossfire Hurricane* operation to surveil the Trump campaign, will go down as the worst scandal in American history. Yet it is hard to credit this scandal with simply being the result of individual actors who suddenly decided to do nefarious things. There has to be a broader context. Without going into the realm of conspiracy theories, we have to touch upon whether or not the influences of the Frankfurt School, the Alinsky and Marcuse influences, the general deconstructionist philosophies of the Left impacted how this all unfolded. How imperative were those ideologues and ideologies to getting to where we arrived with this scandal?

VDH: The way I look at it, Sebastian, is, in a general way, they enhanced the sort of arrogance of these people, these progressive social warriors. And they saw a chance for sixteen years of Obama and Hillary that would transform the nation. The details of how that noble crusade was to be effected were not as important as the crusade itself. And that gave these people like Peter Strzok, or James Comey, or John Brennan, many of whom are just bureaucratic careerists, a sense of impunity or exemption from accountability.

And then the other thing that's more banal, and here you have got to go back to the time of 2016, when everybody was saying that Donald Trump was going to wreck the Republican party, that he had no chance, he would not get the nomination, and if he got it, he would not be elected, and if he got elected, he would destroy the country.

So, there's a sense that, as an "insurance policy," to quote FBI Deputy Director Andrew McCabe, they could do all these things since Hillary was going to be president. And, given her reputation, what would otherwise be illegal behavior would be rewarded as service to a noble cause. These people were really in a competition to prove to future president-elect Hillary that they were responsible for her landslide mandate. And once you start looking at the whole thing in that prism or that matrix, then it makes a lot more sense. It explains why these people were so, not just arrogant, but so careless in the manner in which they operated. I mean after all, Bruce Ohr—how could the fourth-ranking person in the DOJ think he could get away with having his wife work for Glenn Simpson [co-founder of Fusion GPS, which hired Christopher Steele to compose the "dossier" on Donald Trump], and then channel that material all on their side into the FBI? And then not even report that on a federal form about his wife's employment?

It's an arrogance in deluding the FISA courts. There was not even an attempt to cover it up because they were certain that they were morally right, that Hillary Clinton would appreciate their conspiratorial obedience and reward them for it.

GORKA: I think this last point is so interesting because very few people ever mention it. There is a propensity, perhaps, on the Right to jump on the "Deep State" and assume an uber-sophisticated conspiracy theory. But there really is not just a level of arrogance, but also a level of dilettantism with these conspirators: that people responsible for counterintelligence at the FBI are having affairs with each other, cheating on their spouses, and then texting inappropriate comments about the president on their government phones. Or when you have President Obama's former national security adviser, Susan Rice, send herself an exculpatory email on Trump's inauguration day stating that President Obama wanted to make sure everything in Comey's and the DOJ's investigation of Russian "collusion" was "done by the book."[5] This really does undergird the analysis that these people are nefarious, but also incompetent, surely.

VDH: Absolutely. And after all, why would Andy McCabe think that after his wife was a recipient of this nearly $700,000 in Clinton-sourced PAC money, he would not, just a few weeks later, have to recuse himself of investigating her emails? Or why would Hillary Clinton think that she could destroy 33,000 emails under subpoena and destroy the devices they were on, and think she would get away with it?

There was something about the attitude of the country in 2015 and 2016. You really have to remember that Obama had kind of checked out and that his core popularity had gone up because people liked the *idea* of Obama as president, not the *reality* of it. And Hillary was supposedly the sober and judicious Democratic stalwart whose time had come. Everybody was jumping on her bandwagon to prove that they were more loyal than the next, and they would do a better job than the other.

And then Trump was such an outsider, an outlier, and that's the climate in which this all took place. And so they weren't careful, they were arrogant, they were sloppy. But they were also nefarious because deep down inside, they felt that they had the right to act against the Constitution of the United States. They tried to destroy a campaign, they tried to destroy a presidential transition, and then they tried to destroy a presidency.

GORKA: How much was this a function of their belief that Donald Trump could not be president, and that when sixty-three million Americans chose him, they chose the "wrong candidate"?

VDH: Well, I think almost all of it was. And remember that almost immediately, we had an effort in three states to sue to overturn the results—they said the voting machines were corrupt. But that didn't work. And then we had, on Inauguration Day, all those protests—Madonna saying she wanted to blow up the White House. Then there were Articles of Impeachment. And there was that appeal earlier to the electors of the Electoral College not to follow their mandate, that they should be renegades and deny Trump the White House. And then we have flirtation with the Logan Act, and then we have flirtation with the emoluments clause, then the Twenty-fifth Amendment. They even got a Yale psychiatrist to testify. And then, finally, we have the Mueller investigation, and we have the pseudo-coup plan of McCabe and Rod Rosenstein.

So there were a series of efforts to destroy the Trump administration, and they were all based on the idea that this cannot stand because these are not the right people to be in the positions of power. They're not at the Brookings Institution, they're not on the Council of Foreign Relations, they're not from the Economics department at Harvard. These are just crazy people, and we don't want them around. And this was not just the left-wing reaction; there were a lot of prominent Republican Bush-ites who felt the same way.

GORKA: Professor, you've outlined for us the depth and the breadth of the corruption, the conspiracy that really was an attempt, a repeated attempt at a silent coup against a presidential candidate and then a president of the United States. As an American, as an observer, as a commentator, Professor Hanson, what do you think it will take for the American people to regain their trust in those institutions that have such incredible power: the intelligence community and law enforcement?

VDH: I think three things. First, all of the documents, the relevant documents, the millions of pages accumulated during the Russiagate investigations have to be released without redactions. Very few redactions are justified in national security. A few are, but not as many as we're seeing. We have to have the corpus of literature out there. And then second, we've got to get away from this idea of invoking another special counsel, another Patrick Fitzgerald; we have to have confidence in the Department of Justice.

GORKA: I couldn't concur more—the special counsel is a dangerous weapon, whoever the president is.

VDH: It is. So what we need is for Attorney General Barr to go systematically, in a transparent fashion, through what is already on the record. Take for example James Comey. Did he lie under oath on two hundred fifty occasions when he said, "I don't know, I can't remember"? Was it a felony or not a felony to release probably classified memos of presidential conversations? Did he mislead the president when he said, "You're not under investigation?" Did he mislead a FISA court by knowingly withholding the information that the documentation that he was using to get a court order for surveillance was paid for by Hillary Clinton? And if these things are true, then we have to have an open discussion and indictment. And all of these people need to be held accountable. And I could go on and on, but we don't have the time, this applies to Comey, Brennan, McCabe....

GORKA: But do people have to go to jail, Professor Hanson?

VDH: Well, they have to follow the law, Sebastian. So, with what James Comey did, or what James Clapper did, if they are felons, if they are guilty of felonious behavior, and they're convicted, yes. We've already gone where there are no consequences. The reason that we're here is because John Brennan, to take one example, lied on two occasions under oath to the U.S. Senate. Once about surveilling computers of staffers, and once about collateral damage. And Brennan admitted that he lied to the congressional investigation, and nothing happened.

And that gave them a sense of emboldenment that they were set, and I could say the same thing about Susan Rice and her unmasking of people. It's illegal to unmask, not to unmask per se, but to unmask and leak those names to the press, and we know that happened. We don't know why Samantha Power was making hundreds of requests to unmask people.

GORKA: As a U. N. Ambassador who isn't technically part of the intelligence community, that's the remarkable thing. Do you have confidence, Professor Hanson, that Attorney General Barr will try and see justice done?

VDH: I do believe that he will, but I'm not sure that even his integrity and skill and jurisprudence can overcome a very biased federal court system and a Deep State bureaucratic apparatus within the Department of Justice. He's got to deal not just with his own people, but the court system itself, and judges who feel that social justice is a higher calling than the actual letter of the law. So I'm not confident that any of these people will end up, if convicted, and if found guilty, facing the consequences that you or I would face had we been in this situation.

GORKA: We have to wonder whether Lady Justice does indeed still wear a blindfold. Professor, let me touch upon the central theme of your book, *The Case for Trump.* I tend to agree with General Mike Flynn, whom I served with in the Presidential Transition Team and then in the White House, that on November 8, 2016, we saw a peaceful political revolution in the United States. Donald Trump would not have been possible, in my opinion, were it not for the abject failure, the moral and technical bankruptcy, of the "elite" on both Left and Right.

Recently, in Wilkes-Barre, Pennsylvania, President Trump gave a rally speech where he said basically that the elite is dead, and he pointed at the audience and said, "*You* are the super elite."

Professor Hanson, is the "elite" dead in America?

VDH: Well, maybe the current elite. I mean there's always going to be an elite in every society. It may be the elite as we came to view it in the post-war order that is gone. That is, the Ivy League elite, the corporate elite, the globalist elite, I think they've lost a lot of prestige. And on the major issues of our times, they've been on the wrong side. On the illegal immigration mess that we see today, for instance, they were either on the Left, hoping illegal immigration and changing demographics would enhance their power, and or they were on the Right and supporting illegal immigration because they thought cheap labor was good for business. They misread the American people, and they were discredited.

And what you're seeing now with China is the elite in the corporate world and on the so-called "humanitarian Left" scrambling and, without evoking the word "Trump," trying to emulate Trump's tough approach. I mean, where did this come from, as far as China? It's only possible because Trump threw a hammer at the glass, and now they're all suspicious of China. It's the same thing with Iran, Obama's Iran Deal. Trump disrupted a lot of assumed status quo pretensions, and people were bewildered because orthodoxy said, "You can't do that, and if you do, chaos will ensue." And not only did chaos not ensue, but foreign policy and economic successes did. And now they're either trying to piggyback on it or deprecate Trump's contributions, but whatever they're doing, the message is that they could not do that, or they would not do that. And people started to grasp that.

GORKA: Let's talk about President Trump as commander in chief and his strategic impact. In the geopolitical landscape, how significant is it that we now have a president who doesn't come from the "elite" Washington bubble, and who isn't a former politician?

VDH: I think, to sum it up, Trump looks at situations and evaluates them empirically. Is this working? Is this in the United States' interests? Will this advance our allies' or our own agendas? And then he makes his decision on that basis. So if you tell Donald Trump, "Don't dare move our embassy to Jerusalem because you've got a lot of experts on the Middle East who say that will cause another Intifada," he'll wonder what empirical proof the experts have for that assumption. Or if they say, "You cannot decertify the Palestinians as refugees," he's more likely to say something like, "Are they refugees? Are Germans from the Sudetenland still refugees? Are Jews who were ethnically cleansed out of Egypt in 1956 still refugees?" He's looking at the world empirically, and they're not. Yet, they think that they are. So they got into double and triple and quadruple double think, or counterintuitive or counterfactual thinking; they got to the point of over-studying and over-analyzing everything, where an outsider could look at the situation empirically. The so-called experts got into the habit of making deals for the sake of making deals, like Obama's Iranian deal, which allowed the Iranians to make a lot of money and keep up their technology—and then maybe spring a bomb on us in ten years.

It's the same thing with the "climate change" Paris Accord. It was just a mechanism to restrain the United States economically and transfer wealth to other powers. When it comes to energy, we can get by on our own with natural gas or fracking. Trump looked at this deal the way anybody would who had been in the real world and had to make a payroll, and he knew that if a building didn't pencil out, he was going to lose money. But when you're dealing with this bureaucratic mind, a public employee mind, an academic mind, they're not subject to the ramifications of their own ideology. There's no downside. And they're wrong a lot. And then nobody really pays.

GORKA: You make it sound—your description really is redolent of the Hans Christian Andersen story of the naked emperor. Along comes somebody who is not beholden to the court, and he just says, "They've got no clothes on." Is that a fair analogy for the president?

VDH: Yes, I think so. I think I've used that even. Nobody ever in their right mind—the establishment or whatever—would think empirically about Kim Jong-un, to take one example. They think, "He's so volatile; he's so crazy," and they deal with him out of fear. Trump says basically, "Look, I've got a bigger button. We've got all of these nuclear advantages, we've got missile defense, we've got our allies, and we can't establish a situation where this thug threatens us with six or seven nuclear weapons. And so, I'm going to reply in kind." And that was just a heresy. And, yet, it's in line with human nature. Once Kim saw that Trump had the wherewithal to back up his threats, he decided he wanted to talk. And Trump was wise enough to give Kim a carrot by saying we wouldn't forcibly unify the Koreas through military force. That provided an avenue that didn't exist before for a future deal.

I think that Trump is all about the art of the deal. His methodology is to go in, threaten and bluster, and demand three times more than what he would probably settle for, and then scale back and end up with more than anyone thought that he could get.

Look at what President Trump has been doing with the Chinese over the last two years. He's threatening, he's tightening up the tariffs, he's waiting for them to stew in their own juice, and he's not going to cave to them. He slaps $200 billion in tariffs on China and then threatens to raise it to $340 billion if the Chinese don't accept trade reform. But he will allow them to save face with compromises of his own and will get a huge victory because China needs our market more than we need theirs. Nobody in the foreign policy establishment has been thinking like that. But if they did, they would realize that nothing President Trump has done is crazy.

GORKA: How significant is President Trump's impact on the global establishment, the international "elite" that has dominated how politics is done since the end of the Cold War?

VDH: He's made enormous inroads with the EU and NATO. He's set the new rules of the game and is basically saying, "You are a very wealthy, affluent continent, and we're here to help you. But we're not going to subsidize your defense at the same level—it's still subsidized—but not at the same level that you're accustomed to." President Trump has set the new standards of behavior in the relationship. And I think that's positive. He's done the same thing with China. He's telling China that we're no longer going to allow you to have these asymmetrical advantages. That was a very radical thing. So Trump's already made enormous changes in the establishment community, from Silicon Valley to Washington, which had been completely complacent with the Chinese.

GORKA: Has President Trump changed America's political culture for good—or only for the duration of his presidency?

VDH: The problem that Trump is facing is that he is trying to set an example by sheer performance. That's why I think Peter Thiel and some of Trump's supporters are trying to create a commensurate intellectual movement. What Trump does is say, "This is what I did with China, and therefore, this is the model from now on. This is what I did to reindustrialize the Midwest; that's the model. This is what I did on fair trade." And he's doing that partly because he's more of an activist than a theorist, but partly because he's orphaned, or he's alienated, ostracized by the establishment and doesn't have a kitchen cabinet of theorists to memorialize his presidency.

This is the first time we've ever had a president, where the flagship—so-called flagship—magazines, journals, think tanks, councils, they're all anti-Trump. So, there's no effort to go and recruit from those areas. He needs to say to the Republican party, "In the last six elections, we haven't had a 51 percent national party since George H. W. Bush in 1988 beat Dukakis; and we haven't won the popular vote in the last five of the six national elections, and that came at a time when we picked up a thousand seats just to take the Obama administration alone. So until this midterm, we've been successful at the state and local level. But there's something lacking in that wealthy, multi-million-dollar, white, male Romney, McCain, Dole, two Bushes profile that we gravitate to. That comes out of a particular background and cannot appeal to lower middle-class and working-class 'deplorables' in nine or ten states—which are still going to be absolutely essential for electoral success, even with a so-called changed demography."

So, I think, what I'm getting at is they're going to have to really study in depth the Trump position on immigration, trade, manufacturing, and a lot of that is antithetical Milton Friedman, free-market "creative destruction." And, yet, that Milton Friedman model gets you no more than 46 percent of the popular vote, which isn't enough unless you have a really bad candidate running against you.

GORKA: So, unless the conservative establishment embraces the nascent Trump Doctrine, or the MAGA model, his incredibly significant and positive effect will be ephemeral, is what you're saying?

VDH: Yes. In 2024, you will see candidates like Cruz, or Rubio, maybe, half-heartedly emulate his nationalist themes—but not to Trump's extent or success. The irony is that they criticize Trump for being crude and callous, but his approach is far more empathetic and caring about people than is this abstract creative-destruction, Republican orthodoxy. You really saw that with Paul Ryan—the way that an inept Joe Biden beat him in the 2012 vice-presidential televised debate. He was pathetic because he just relied on all of these, sort of free-market, think tank nostrums, and Biden just talked about people in a very adolescent way, but it still came off as better than what Ryan had to say.

GORKA: And the president's empathy derives from his desire to help working-class Americans get their jobs back, correct?

VDH: I think so. I've talked to a lot of people about that. And whether it's personal that he's done these building deals where he saw the actual people who were building them, and he had to actually deal with the unions and workers—whether it came from that, or whether it came from having a chip on his shoulder about being a Queens outsider, or whether he developed a natural difference of opinion from the financiers and bankers and investors about interest rates, economic growth, unions, and nationalism. He's not a globalist. He's a pragmatic economic nationalist less interested in high-interest rates and making money without actual, visible, tangible results than he is about jobs that matter to working people. Trump is definitely about manufacturing, production, farming, mining, timber, and not the hedge fund, global insurance, high-tech world where the big money now is. I don't think Romney or McCain could have said as passionately as Trump does that our miners, our vets, our farmers are important.

GORKA: Yes, and he means it. He really means it.

VDH: If he's going to get reelected—and save the Republican party—he's going to have to emphasize that sincere passion. He's also very effective when he's self-deprecatory. I wish he would emphasize that more because it makes him much more complex and really confuses his enemies. He can be very funny in a weird way.

The problem is that they create such a 360-degree pressure front around him: media, foundations, universities, activists, Hollywood, entertainment, television, that he's in 24/7 combat mode. And he feels that to let down his guard would be to lose deterrence and only incur more attacks. But, at some point, he's going to have to risk being more—as I said—self-critical and funny. He can do it very well, which is ironic.

GORKA: Given the scope of your expertise, historically, is there a character from history who is a close analogue to the impact that this non-politician, this outsider, has had on the elites? Is there someone who comes to mind who is similar to Trump?

VDH: Well, that answer would entail two aspects. One, is there anybody who, whatever his background was, came into power on the idea that national or civilizational decline was not fated, but is a matter of choice? You can really see somebody like that in the Emperor Justinian.

The Empire was lost in the west. The demography wasn't good. The enemies were surrounding the Byzantine Empire, and yet he basically had to "make Byzantium great again," and he went in and conquered North Africa; he invaded Sicily; he took over two-thirds of Italy; he got to some degree into Spain, into Thrace; he codified the Justinian code of law; he crushed the decadent establishment in Byzantium; he crushed the blues and the greens—the so-called sports gangs who were actually subversives—and he unleashed some really talented generals with Narses and especially Belisarius. So, he was a guy who basically said, "It's not twilight for the Eastern Empire. All of the ingredients of stability and progress are still here. We have just psychologically given into the idea that we have to follow the decline and fall of the Western Empire." And he did have a very different background. He didn't speak Greek at all. He grew up in parts of Western Europe that were

Latin, north of the Danube, near Romania. So, he was a real outsider-guy, and he brought a lot of outsiders with him.

So, for me, Trump is somebody like that—an outsider intent on really changing things. And he may well succeed. Whatever we think about Justinian, his legacy lasted for a thousand years.

GORKA: And the other aspect?

VDH: The first aspect is not so much the agenda but the nature of the historical figure, an Augustus or Justinian, who feels that they can—by sheer force of will—convince their people that the problem is in their minds, not in the stars. This kind of man is just so different, like Napoleon, a two-bit Corsican artillery officer, who does not have the pedigree of any of the French military elite.

Nobody quite knew how to square the circle of creating a revolutionary egalitarianism without at the same time destroying the institutions necessary for French nationalism. And then in a brilliant fashion Napoleon basically says, "My marshals of France are going to be meritocratic; even if they're aristocrats, they're going to have to compete, and my spoils and the laurels of victory are going to go to people along the lines of revolutionary egalitarianism," even though he was an authoritarian-nationalist. He was a complete outsider; linguistically, ethnically, he was not a part of the French elite, and he capitalized on that. And, so, we've had these people—we've had two presidents actu-ally, Ulysses S. Grant and Dwight D. Eisenhower—who never had any political experience, but they did have mili-tary experience. What's unique about Trump is that he's the first president to have neither political nor military experience, and nobody thought that'd be possible. And I think we'll see a lot of people on the other side especially, who will think that they can emulate Trump's ability.

GORKA: Let me drill down on that. How tectonic a change to our political culture was the election of 2016? Some have posited that the Deplorables' election of Donald Trump has broken the stranglehold of the Brookings Insti-tution types, the know-it-alls, the op-ed writers. Do you agree? Or will we snap back after a second term of Donald Trump to business as usual? How large is the impact, his-torically, of the 2016 election?

VDH: I think it's pretty large, because there have been these force multipliers like the Internet, like blogging, like Twitter, that allow messaging to go out regardless of the elite. It doesn't matter anymore. You can see it in the Democratic party. As popular leaders you've got a seventy-seven-year-old socialist in Bernie Sanders and a twenty-nine-year-old basically know-nothing in AOC. Most of the other party's presidential candidates worry the Democratic establishment. The whole thing is in flux. On the Republican side, I don't think people will care if Mitt Romney or Jeb Bush wades in, or the Koch brothers, or George Will or Bill Kristol—these were the voices of the sober and judicious Republican establishment. I don't think anybody in Michigan or Pennsylvania or the Central Valley of California listens to them anymore.

People have tuned them out because they cried wolf one too many times. "Trump is a monster, Trump can't be the nominee, Trump can't be elected, Trump can't succeed." After a while, people think, "Just go away." And I think that's the attitude they have towards a lot of these people.

Maybe we could have a more meritocratic elite where the track record of your actual performance mattered more than where you went to school or the letters behind your name. That would be welcome, but there's always going to be an elite. I just hope it's not an East Coast, West Coast, corporate, media, university elite.

GORKA: Well, I think it's clear that he's broken the "Never-Trumpers," that he has made them increasingly irrelevant; however, it seems there has been no change in the Left. If you look at the language of Democrats, they talk of concentration camps in America, ICE needing to be disbanded, and the president's re-election campaign launch being analogous to a Nazi Nuremburg rally. Does this mean, Professor Hanson, that things will get worse on the Left before they get better?

VDH: Yes, because when we say "elite," there are different types of roles that an elite can play. In the case of the Democratic party, because they were interested in political power, a Dianne Feinstein or a Joe Biden or a Chuck Schumer tried to mask or camouflage the insidious progressivism that was growing in their party. And now that elite is discredited, and you and I are talking about AOC or Representative Ilhan Omar, Elizabeth Warren, Kamala Harris, or Bernie Sanders. We're not talking about Chuck Schumer or John Kerry, or all these supposed senior statesmen in the Democratic party; they're completely irrelevant now. There's been a Jacobin revolution on the Left, and you've got street fighters and brawlers and baristas. You've got everybody in there.

In one way, I like to see it. I'm not a fan of the progressive movement. But on the other hand, you can see what happens when their gatekeepers are overwhelmed by the mob, and the mob is in the street, and that's what's happening in the Democratic party.

GORKA: Given the grim, grim things we already know about how power was abused relentlessly and repeatedly during the Obama administration for political purposes, especially to spy on candidate Trump and President Trump, knowing all that, as an American, do you feel optimistic about our future as a Republic, or do you think that we are Rome on the edge of collapse?

VDH: Well, you know, Rome took four hundred years for a splintered decline. What I'm more worried about is the largest number of immigrants we've ever seen, not that I dislike immigration, but we're not assimilating and integrating them. We're substituting ideas of social justice for the rule of law: if your motives are deemed noble by progressives, then you can do anything. That said, I think that when Americans are given the information, the choice, they're not going to vote for reparations or infanticide or the Green New Deal or the wealth tax or abolishing the Electoral College or student debt or ICE or free college for everyone. I don't think they're ready for that yet. And I think there's going to be a pushback.

But at these critical points in American history, whether it's instituting a draft on the heels of Pearl Harbor, it's never been a sure thing. And, you know, the Confederate Army was on its way to southern Ohio until it fought Union forces at Shiloh, and on the first day it almost won. So, you've come very close to catastrophe in our history. And we're dealing with it now, but we just have to hope that the common sense of the American public will prevail.

☐ ☐ ☐

Now to our second observer of the radical Left and the Trump Effect. Lord Black, or Conrad Moffat Black, Baron Black of Crossharbour, is one of a dying breed. Born in Canada, Conrad Black epitomizes a bygone era, one populated by truly larger-than-life characters, incredibly successful men who could make fortunes in business, whilst discoursing on the finer details of the history of Western Civilization and penning biographies of American presidents.

Lord Black is a legendary figure in the media world as well, having at one time or another owned the *Chicago Sun-Times*, the UK's *Daily Telegraph*, the *Spectator*, the *Jerusalem Post*, and Canada's *National Post*. At the same time, he has suffered at the hands of an overzealous American prosecutor, just as President Trump did during the Mueller investigation. In Lord Black's case, however, he fell victim to said prosecutor, eventually serving time in jail for an alleged crime that President Trump pardoned him for shortly after I interviewed him. Now read what a businessman, media mogul, and historian has to say about the challenges that you, I, and the president face.

> **GORKA:** Lord Black, you are a very successful businessman in the world of finance, but also a historian, a man of letters who's written incredibly successful books on Roosevelt and Nixon. Not only that, you are uniquely positioned as a businessman and historian to write living history, because you have actually negotiated with Donald Trump the businessman.

> **BLACK:** Oh indeed. That was twenty years ago. And that was how I first knew him, in a business context.

> **GORKA:** So this gives you a unique perspective, a perspective that has led you in your most recent book, *Donald J. Trump: A President Like No Other*, to describe our

president as a "popular tribune," which doesn't very much fit into modern Judeo-Christian Western politics. That phrase harkens back to maybe the age of the Founding Fathers or back to the original Roman Republic. What do you mean by popular tribune?

BLACK: By that I mean he represents the authentic voice of a widespread sentiment among average people—and that is, on its face, very surprising for a man who is, by a wide margin, the wealthiest man ever to be the president of the United States. But to a degree, you could say the same thing about Franklin D. Roosevelt, except that he made no pretense about being an average person anyway and was clearly quite satisfied to be a very patrician figure, with an elegant and educated accent. Donald Trump has an "outer borough" accent, though you can tell that he is an educated man, even if his detractors pretend that you cannot and that he isn't.

But he does rather sound like a middle-class, or even working-class person much of the time. He is authentic, and as with Roosevelt, you can't tell where he came from. As you've kindly said, I wrote a book about Franklin D. Roosevelt, and no one could ever figure out how he had the genius of knowing where public opinion was at all times, but he did. And so with Donald Trump. He got out among the people to an astonishing degree, in the commotion of wrestling matches and prize fights and as a television star. But even so, he's an extremely wealthy man, proud of being a wealthy man, and yet he intuitively, and tactically, successfully appeals to the legitimate sentiments, not the prejudices, of a very, very large number of Americans—I would say now probably more than half of the population.

GORKA: As an individual who worked for him in the White House I've seen this man connect as a billionaire, as a president, with steel workers in Steel Valley, Youngstown, Ohio. How does that happen? How does an individual of his wealth, an individual who lives in the rarified atmosphere of private jumbo jets, how does he resonate with steel workers, Lord Black?

BLACK: Every summer he worked for his father on building sites, his father being a developer also. And he managed some sites when he started, not the work crews, but he was intimately involved in the real nuts and bolts of that business, to the point where he could mix the pest control fluids to get rid of roaches and things like that. And he always knew the working man. That's where it came from.

He always knew those people, he has a very gregarious personality, and that comes across quite clearly. I think his enemies can't dispute that. They may claim that he is not the sort of person that they would wish to associate with, but you can see that he is very affable and so on. He has that very extensive background working shoulder-to-shoulder with working-class and middle-class people, and he knows what their concerns are.

And he never—even at the height of his activities as a successful businessman—he was never around very much the Park Avenue, 5th Avenue, traditional elite, the social elite. You would see him, yes (and I was slightly in that circuit for a time, and lived part of the time in New York, and he was a neighbor of ours in New York and Palm Beach, in a rather grander combination of places he had close by). You'd see him in these big evening events for many charities in New York sometimes, but you'd never see him in the halls of 5th Avenue or Park Avenue as a guest; he was always busy.

I got to know him through business, and then somewhat socially, but he was busy all the time, with his television or his business. And he was not interested in hob-knobbing with the rich, which is the normal ambition of people who make a lot of money in New York, you know, they want to fraternize with other wealthy and socially prominent people.

GORKA: There are theories of history that present what I think is a false dichotomy in terms of whether it's circumstance that creates the leader, or leaders are born and then they change history. You, however, have written about the "elitist decay," about the conditions of self-hatred and ideological determinism that America became hostage to prior to the last presidential election. Is Donald Trump's presidency a reaction to the eight years of Obama and the political neo-Marxism of the last forty years? Or, knowing him as you do, was his election inevitable?

BLACK: First, on the argument that you opined, both happened at different times. Sometimes circumstances create the man or person, and sometimes it's the other way around. And I'm not an apostle of the "Great Man Theory," but it does have some validity. There is no question, between Winston Churchill and Franklin D. Roosevelt, that they really saved Western Civilization by providing the leadership they did. In the case of Donald Trump, I think he saw it coming, and he watched it grow—the frustration and the irritation of a very large number of what we might just call ordinary Americans, traditionally called the working class and middle class.

And he was always polling, because he was always interested in the idea of translating celebrity into high office. And you may recall that he was in the primaries as a candidate for the nomination of the Reform party in 2000. He won primaries in Michigan and California, but then he concluded, quite correctly, that historically third parties never win in the United States. Not even Theodore Roosevelt could do it in the famous election of the three presidents, against Taft and Wilson in 1912.

And so he was waiting for his moment, and he changed parties seven times in thirteen years; he's not a party loyalist. He was waiting for this moment to develop and to perfect his technique. And at pulling twenty-five million viewers at least every week for fifteen years, an astounding record, and getting into these improbable places for normal politicians, like 90,000 people in the Silverdome to watch him shear the hair off Vince McMahon of the wrestling federation. He was always angling for it and watching the level of discontent grow.

So he was the beneficiary, not just of the failings of the Obama Administration, but of the preceding administrations. I put it to you, Sebastian, that the twenty years preceding Donald Trump were the worst twenty years in government in the history of this country. I would accept that the presidents immediately prior to the Civil War were less competent presidents than Obama and George W. Bush, but they didn't go on as long.

But from the late Clinton era all the way through George W. Bush and Obama, we got the policies that produced the greatest economic crisis in the world since the Great Depression.

We got an endless war in the Middle East, the chief result of which was to hand effective control of most of Iraq to Iran, which is exactly the reverse of what was intended and an immense humanitarian crisis.

We got a flatlined economy. Gross domestic product per capita growth went from 4 percent and 4.5 percent under Reagan, to 3.9 percent under Clinton, to 2 percent under the second Bush, to 1 percent under Obama.

And the country was like a pressure-cooker, but the media didn't notice it. The system worked for the rich friends of the regimes, and it worked for Hollywood, and it worked for Silicon Valley. But the average American, the backbone of the nation, felt they were being left out. And Trump saw that when nobody else did.

GORKA: There are those such as Steve Bannon, and others, who have said that politics, Left and Right, means nothing anymore. We are now in the age of dueling populisms, the leftist populism of Bernie Sanders and Alexandria Ocasio-Cortez versus Donald Trump, Brexit, Italy's Northern League, and the Brazilian populism of President Bolsorano. Is it that simple, number one, has politics so radically changed? And second, after his second term, will Donald Trump have effected some permanent change on the body politic or will power merely return to the establishment elite of the fetid swamp?

BLACK: Well, I think there will be a durable change, Sebastian. I wouldn't put it exactly as you did, citing Steve Bannon, but I do think the Left-Right thing is getting quite blurred. And I think most serious conservatives would not concede that the Left has a monopoly, for example, on the concern for civil rights. And most moderate Leftists would object to being labeled as totally fiscally irresponsible, or pacifists, or the like.

I think what the country wants, and what all democratic countries want, is policies that work. People do become extremely resentful of complacent elites who set things up very nicely for themselves but leave the working class and the middle class living paycheck to paycheck or living off state benefits. And you know, that's been a widespread phenomenon, and you see it in all the advanced Western countries now.

But I think on your second point, that yes, the Trump presidency will have a durable impact. I think Reagan left the country in good shape, and the problem was that George Bush Sr. allowed Ross Perot to split the Republicans, take twenty million mainly Republican votes, and bring on the Clintons. And then things started to go downwards, and they went down at a steeper and steeper angle for the succeeding years. Trump won because of what had preceded him. But I think he will redirect the country again to the virtues of low taxes, relative deregulation, and a serious definition of the American national interest that is enforceable and doesn't over-extend the country.

Given the increasing rate of change, it would be hazardous to predict that his impact would be permanent, but I think it'll be durable.

GORKA: But for it to be durable, to quote my friend Monica Crowley, we need more people like Donald Trump who truly aren't ideological, at least in the taxonomy we've used in the past, but are "attitudinal" in terms of their practical behavior and their love of country. Is there a class of people who are prepared, who have the celebrity, who have the wherewithal, the spine, to create a new political class that is less ideological and more attitudinal, Conrad Black?

BLACK: I think so. I think so. You see, I've felt that was one of the greatest assets of America. When the northeastern establishment, the Ivy League and Wall Street, really dropped the ball in Vietnam, they pushed Lyndon Johnson into it while they all fled thereafter into the long grass—the best and the brightest, the Kennedy leftovers. As that happened, a new group, mainly from California, led by Ronald Reagan, came in with the optimism of the American West, and took their place.

And what we have now, I think, is a kind of completely non-violent but militant common-sense, middle-class, fact-based movement here. It isn't reactionary, it isn't in any sense retrograde, although it's presented as such. And this kind of movement says, "Let's get rid of this phony regime where there's this masquerade of caring about the little people while, in fact, everything is taken care of for Wall Street and Hollywood and Silicon Valley, but not for the country."

Most Americans, despite the horrible problems in academia, are fiercely patriotic, they love the country, they're proud of the country, and they want it to do well. And they're right to be proud, but they're also right to recognize that there are terrible problems that have to be dealt with.

GORKA: I, as a proud American, now of seven years, I've always said that of the many common characteristics of my fellow Americans, the central one is common sense. And thanks to you Lord Black we may have found a new label for what "Trumpism" is, "militant common sense." A militant common sense alloyed to an unswerving love of country and belief in America.

□　□　□

Thus, the insights of two great observers of the American scene: Victor Davis Hanson and Conrad Black. The question we now face is whether we can stop the leftists who are trying to sabotage President Trump's *Make America Great Again* mission and whether President Trump can win reelection in 2020. I believe, as you'll see, that, with your help, it can be done.

CHAPTER FIVE

HOW YOU CAN WIN THE WAR FOR AMERICA'S SOUL

A s you can see, they have a plan. The radical fringe of the Democrat party, the extremists of the 1960s and 1970s have become
the "mainstream." Bernie Sanders, an avowed Socialist who
honeymooned in the Soviet Union,[1] almost won the Democrat nomination for president in 2016 (only to have Hillary Clinton steal it with
her "superdelegates."), and the old radicals have now been reinforced
by the product of fifty years of left-wing indoctrination in our schools
and colleges, exemplified by Alexandria Ocasio-Cortez. And now,
thanks to an acquiescent and obsequious media, their extremist views
are parroted openly, including the need to abolish ICE and the Department of Homeland Security, as AOC and her subservient colleagues

brazenly promote communism under the cover of Environmentalism with a "Green New Deal" that would ban gas-powered cars, air travel, and beef husbandry as we know it today, and require the destruction and reconstruction of all the homes and commercial buildings in America in order to make them "environmentally friendly." This would require a Communist level of government control—and that is the level of control over your lives that the Democrat party wants to have. If we let them.

We know what our political enemies want and what they have been assiduously working for since the late 1960s. So we have satisfied, according to conventional wisdom, the first task of any war, which is the Chinese strategist Sun Tzu's admonition to "know your enemy." Sun Tzu is a person that people like to show off their familiarity with; if you go to a fancy cocktail party, somebody will try to drop his name when they're discussing strategy. Yet he is almost always misquoted. What everybody can tell you is, "Oh, yes, Sun Tzu, the master of strategy said, 'You must know your enemy in order to defeat him!'" But it's not that simple. If you know your enemy, you will only be victorious in half your battles. The original quote is "If you know the enemy and know yourself, you need not fear the result of a hundred battles. If you know yourself but not the enemy, for every victory gained you will also suffer a defeat. If you know neither the enemy nor yourself, you will succumb in every battle."[2] And this is our biggest problem now, our biggest problem as conservatives, and our biggest problem as a civilization since the 1960s: we do not know who we are, and we've allowed those who actually have disdain for our civilization to gain control of our culture.

We've forgotten how to win, not only because we have far too often lost the will to fight, but because we've forgotten how to tell stories that express what we're fighting for. You win in politics because your story is better. That's modern politics. It's not just about having the facts. The Gipper was the master politician, in the positive sense of the word. Why? Because he knew the truth, *and* he knew how to communicate it. The "amiable dunce"[3] that we were told was President Ronald Reagan, spent years before he became governor of California traveling the nation, going from GE factory to GE factory, lecturing American workers and managers, the backbone of this nation, on why our Republic is so great, and why a free-market constitutional democracy is the greatest economic and political gift to mankind.

He gave hundreds of such lectures to the American people, and he wrote each one himself. So when he finally became president, what did he bring to that position? He had all the facts at his fingertips, but he didn't, as is so often the case on our side, just regale his audience with the facts. He didn't just give them statistics and quotes from von Mises and Hayek or Burke until people started snoring. He communicated the truth of those eternal verities as a talented Hollywood actor can, by telling stories. He combined the truth with a capacity to connect emotionally with his audience.

This is what we forget. One more policy paper, one more full-page ad in a newspaper makes not one whit of difference. Not one whit. And the conservative movement has wasted literally billions of dollars on the wrong things for decades now. If only we had listened to the wisdom of one man, the late Andrew Breitbart. *Righteous Indignation* is the most important book I have read in the last twenty years. And I read a lot. It offers his own superb description of the roots of the far Left and his own heroic struggle against its growing influence.

But beyond his book and the website he founded, the most important thing about Andrew—and this is why we owe him such a great debt—is that he, in one sentence, in one constantly repeated adage, gave us the road map to victory when he said, "Politics is downstream from culture."[4]

Every morning when we wake up, we must have that emblazoned in front of our eyes. We will never win a political battle on a political battleground, because by the time an issue—whether it's immigration, education, or the right to life—becomes a political hot potato debated on Capitol Hill, it has already been decided in the culture, probably a decade before it became a policy discussion in the Swamp.

You want to know who's to blame for the fact that antisemitic, radical socialists like Ilhan Omar and Alexandria Ocasio Cortez are embraced by the Democrat party? Look in the mirror. Yes, we are to blame. The Left had a plan to dismantle Judeo-Christian civilization from the inside, and we let them. Don't blame a scapegoat. We are responsible for where we are today. And only we can fix it.

I had the high honor of serving Mr. Trump as an advisor during his campaign, and then as a strategist in the White House after he became president. Whatever God you pray to, I can tell you one thing with utter certitude: November 8, 2016, is proof empirical that God exists. We were granted a miracle so that we could try to save our Republic. Let's be clear. Hillary Clinton had it in the bag: $1.4 billion spent, 95 percent of the media in her back pocket, the establishment in her back pocket, and an utter conviction that the prize was hers, that she would become the first woman president. And then what happened?

A man who had never held political office, not at the county level, let alone at the state or federal level, became president of the United

States in his first attempt at elected office. Before Trump, every president of the United States had, in some way, been a product of the political or military establishment, even the changemakers. They had all been previously elected as politicians or been military commanders. And then along comes a guy who had fourteen seasons of a reality TV show.

General Mike Flynn was spot on when he said that what happened in November 2016 was a peaceful political revolution. And everything is on the table in 2020. Everything. Look at what's going on, whether it's freedom of speech, healthcare, education, the Second Amendment, right to life issues—all of it is on the table. The Left even wants to abolish the Department of Homeland Security and Immigration and Customs Enforcement so that we'll have no protection at our national borders, and we become defenseless. They want, in short, to abolish America, and they want to replace our political and economic freedoms, which have made us the greatest country in the world, with the economic and moral failure that is socialism.

Let me make this personal.

It is possible at times to identify moments in your life where everything changes, where a decision point is met and you go down one avenue and not the other, and it changes all. Mine occurred in the south of France when I was about eight years old.

My parents were Hungarians who escaped the Communist regime in Hungary and resettled in Britain, where I was born and raised. But my parents were very worldly, very cultured, and they loved to travel. Every summer we would go abroad, usually to the south of France.

We were on a beach, and I was playing with my Action Men (the British version of G.I. Joes) in the sand, as a child should. My father came out of the ocean from a swim. He had been an amazing athlete, a member of the Hungarian national crew team, and even though the Communists had arrested and imprisoned him, they failed to break him physically, and he was still a huge bear of a man. As I looked at him, I saw something that I hadn't noticed before. I said to my father, "What are those lines on your wrists?"

Without emotion, without skipping a beat, he looked at me and said, "Son, that's where the Secret Police bound my wrists together with wire behind my back so they could hang me from the ceiling of the torture chamber."

That's when my life changed.

From that moment onward, Good and Evil weren't theoretical, abstract concepts. Good and Evil weren't fanciful words from fairy tales about dragons and witches in forests. Good and Evil walked the earth. Evil existed in the hearts of men, men like the Communist officers who had tortured my father in the basement of their headquarters. My father was an anti-Communist student and dissident, arrested, tortured, and imprisoned with a life sentence. Two years in solitary confinement, two years down in the prison coal mine, before he was liberated by the freedom fighters in the glorious but short-lived Hungarian Revolution. And he faced Evil, Evil done by men, Evil that cost the lives—in just the last century—of a hundred million souls.

Read *The Black Book of Communism*, written by a group of European historians, social scientists, and researchers. One of its chief authors, Stéphane Courtois, was himself a former socialist who recanted. Together they catalogued the crimes of communism across the globe, from Russia to Cambodia. And it's all there for you to read. At least one hunded million human beings killed. It is this ideology that has taken hold of the Democrat party, from top to bottom, from "old white men" like Bernie Sanders to young Puerto Rican former bartenders from Brooklyn like Ocasio-Cortez.

I tell you this because the Victims of Communism Memorial Foundation does a poll every year with YouGov, a very serious poll, before their annual gala. Last year's Victims of Communism poll found that 52 percent of American Millennials would prefer to live in a Communist or Socialist America. We have our work cut out for us. I am an American by choice, not by accident. And I'm proud to live in the greatest nation on God's earth. But we have ceded the battlefield. It was one man who didn't need the job, but who took on the challenge as a patriotic duty, who has given us a tiny window to save our Republic. And every single reader of this book has a role to play.

In June of this year, President Trump launched his reelection campaign for 2020 from a stadium in Orlando, and I was there. It was an electrifying evening with twenty-one thousand people inside and thousands more outside, some of whom had lined up more than two days before the event. The night was opened by Lara Trump, then Eric Trump followed with his brother Don Jr. Finally, Vice President Pence spoke and introduced the president and the first lady.

President Trump's speech was perhaps his best ever, and the message was very simple. Halfway through President Trump asked: "What happens if we lose?" Just imagine what happens to the courts, including the Supreme Court, to your right to control your healthcare, to your Second Amendment rights, to a newborn baby's right to life. They want to take it all. Think what will happen if the radical Left wins in 2020. Don't just imagine the horror. Be part of the team that makes President Trump's second victory a reality.

Because I am an American by choice, my default position is optimism because that is what America means to me—we are an optimistic country of freedom and opportunity and success. We must be optimists as Americans. But I have lived in D.C. long enough to know that this is a dark, dark moment, especially when we are honest about what really happened in 2016. Donald J. Trump won despite the GOP. He did not win because of the Republican party, he won despite the Republican party.

And it is a rank, festering indictment of our party that we have more than two hundred men and women on Capitol Hill, meant to represent their districts, meant to represent conservative voters, who have the letter R next to their name, when how many of those official Republicans have had the president's back for the last three years? I'll tell you right now: it's a handful. Matt Gaetz, Devin Nunes, Lindsey Graham, Jim Jordan, Mark Meadows, Lee Zeldin, Louie Gohmert, and a few others. This is their president! This is the man who brought the GOP back from the brink of turning over our future to Hillary Clinton and the socialism of the Democrat party. The rest of the cowardly Republicans should be ashamed of themselves. But they aren't, and as a result, it is for us to put their feet to the fire, to make them afraid for their political future and re-election, and, in the meantime, mobilize everyone around us.

And it's a very simple thing. It doesn't matter where I go. Whether it's a radio event, a book event, a rally, or a lecture. I always say the same thing to everyone: each of you needs to bring ten conservative-minded people who would otherwise not vote to the polling stations. You know the Democrat machine will be organized. You know it will bus people to the polls. We need every single Trump-supporting voter to turn out and cast his or her ballot.

In the meantime, I don't care how old you are, I don't care how cack-handed you consider yourself to be technologically, if you don't have a social media account on Twitter, Facebook, and Instagram, you are not part of the solution, you are part of the problem. It really is that simple. Because there is a reason this man has sixty million Twitter followers—because we ceded the culture, and because the media and information domains belong to them, and the president needs a way to get his word out. CNN cut the coverage of the biggest presidential rally in modern history because the audience started to chant, "CNN sucks." The American people expressed their opinion, spoke the truth, and CNN cut the feed. That's what you do in Venezuela. So, it's up to us to replace Fake News with real news about President Trump's accomplishments. Follow him, retweet him, post instances of the Left's corruption and malfeasance, which is happening all around us all the time, from school boards demanding that elementary school students be exposed to the ideology of "transgenderism" to so-called "sanctuary cities" that harbor criminals and refuse to cooperate with federal law enforcement. We need to be out there with the modern equivalent of a megaphone. Otherwise, we will lose.

There's a very famous Chinese dissident, Chen Guangcheng, a pro-life lawyer who happens to be blind. The Chinese Communist party put him under house arrest, but he escaped. He climbed onto the roof of his shack, walked to the next village, evaded the secret police, and made it hundreds of miles to Beijing where he sought asylum in the American embassy.[5] Because that's who we are: we are the beacon of liberty and hope to the world. But if we don't win in 2020, and we have socialism imposed upon us by the Democrat party, you, dear reader, are not going to have another nation's embassy to run to. That reality, those stakes, are what we need to remember.

Since January 1, 2019, I've been incredibly blessed to be given an incredible national radio show, AMERICA First on the Salem Network. I'm convinced I have the best callers in the industry—they're just absolutely incredible. I'm going to highlight one of my callers as an example of the fortitude we will all have to have to win the political and cultural war we are in.

I had a veteran call in. He was a member of a minority. He'd served his nation and was now in the federal government, and he told me on live radio that his son had been a serviceman, serving multiple tours abroad after the 2001 attacks. He said that after his son's last tour of duty, he came home only to be killed by an illegal alien without a driver's license who crashed his vehicle into him. And this caller said to me, "I'm a veteran, my son served his nation, he's now dead. And I'm not getting a paycheck because the government has shut down. But I want my president to keep the government shut down until the wall is built!"

Do we have that same level of love for our country? Do we have that level of commitment? The most important speech, historically, that the president has given to date was in Warsaw in July 2017. When I was in the White House, we were preparing that speech, and the hosts, the Polish government, wanted President Trump to deliver it in a very fancy palace downtown, and we said no. We said we want the president of the United States to be in the outskirts, by the statue which marks the site of the Warsaw Uprising against the Nazi occupation. We want him right there, next to the statue of freedom fighters, who are seen coming out of the sewers to fight the fascists. Eventually, the Polish government acquiesced.

And that speech is a speech that gives me strength when I read it. And I've read it at least twice on my radio show. Here are the two crucial passages:

> The fundamental question of our time is whether the West has the will to survive. Do we have the confidence in our values to defend them at any cost? Do we have enough respect for our citizens to protect our borders? Do we have the desire and the courage to preserve our civilization in the face of those who would subvert and destroy it?
>
> Our own fight for the West does not begin on the battlefield—it begins with our minds, our wills, and our souls. Today, the ties that unite our civilization are no less vital, and demand no less defense, than that bare shred of land on which the hope of Poland once totally rested. Our freedom, our civilization, and our survival depend on these bonds of history, culture, and memory.

What are you prepared to do to protect our country? Are you prepared to run for local office, volunteer on a campaign, support the president and his team on social media? In comparison to what he has done for you, that would seem the least we could all do. Are you with me? Are you with President Trump?

I'm a legal immigrant to the United States. I chose this country, and I know it to be the greatest country on God's earth. You were likely born here. Will you help me help the president to secure not only your freedom but that of your children and future generations of Americans?

We have to make a principled stand, inform ourselves, and then act. I think that's why you bought and are reading this book. God bless you for it. Everyone who loves America has to stand up for the truth. It is up to us. Every single one of us, and everything we do for the cause of our constitutional Republic, matters. Join us in pushing back against the media's lies and the Democrat party's embrace of tyranny and socialism. President Trump's victory in 2016 gave us a fighting chance, but 2020 is the political battle we cannot afford to lose.

Wherever you see lies, wherever you see political correctness at work, push back with the truth. As Andrew Breitbart taught us, we are all citizen journalists now—and you have more audio and video capability in your pocket than journalists had in their duffle bags twenty years ago, so use it. Together we can save America.

STRAIGHT ANSWERS TO POPULAR QUESTIONS

E ven before I joined the Trump Administration, I was used to
speaking to audiences across the nation. Part of that was my day
job, lecturing to our military and the law enforcement and intelligence communities on the current national security threats we face,
and how to understand our enemies, and how to defeat them. But
since leaving the White House and launching my national radio show,
AMERICA First, I have travelled far and wide to speak to audiences
comprised more of your average patriots, people who want to hear
about my time in the White House, what my old boss "is really like,"
and how we will defeat the increasingly radical scourge that is today's
Democrat party.

Nevertheless, wherever I may be, or whoever is in the audience—and whatever topic the hosts may have given me to speak on—the best part of any event is answering the questions I get from the crowd. It's during the question and answer segment that you find out what people truly care about, what they are most worried about, where they see us heading as a nation, and what advice or words of encouragement they are most eager to hear.

However, I always feel as if I end up shortchanging my fellow Americans since we always run out of time before we run out of questions. Not anymore!

On the next few pages, before you get to my exclusive interview with President Trump, I have collected questions that I have received but never had the chance to address from various engagements, as well as from my *AMERICA First* listeners. Here are the answers to the questions you've always wanted me to answer.

Q: Why did you leave the White House?

GORKA I'm always surprised when people ask me this question—especially conservatives, because it's not a secret. When I resigned, my letter of resignation to the president was published in the press. You can read the full text of it at Breitbart.com. But, in a nutshell, the story is very simple: my job as a White House strategist had essentially been preempted by the president's top national security adviser. I did not work in the National Security Council, I worked in the office of the Chief Strategist, Steve Bannon, in the White House. But once H. R. McMaster replaced General Michael

Flynn as National Security Adviser, my work in the White House became more and more difficult. McMaster clearly did not like me, boxed me out of key decisions, and did not invite me to important meetings. When Steve Bannon resigned in August 2017, I was left in this twilight zone of staying on staff without my immediate boss, doing the odd media hit for the president, and picking up a sizable tax-payer-funded paycheck whilst being undermined by the national security adviser. I decided that it would be immoral to maintain a position where I could no longer be an effective strategist for the president. So, in my letter to President Trump, I made it clear that certain forces not loyal to the "Make America Great Again" agenda were in ascendance in the White House, and, as such, I could more effectively serve the MAGA agenda and the president on the outside of the building—and that is exactly what I've been doing since I left, whether it's with my media appearances, my books, or my new radio show, *AMERICA First*, there is a need to be able to provide the president with full-throated support from the outside, and that's what I've been doing. I've spoken to him since I left, and he appreciates it and he, in fact, has told me that I am more effective without the bureaucrats hanging around my neck.

Fortunately, H. R. McMaster has left, and John Bolton is his replacement—which is very good news for America.

Who knows what the future holds, but right now I'm having far too much fun on the outside of government to think of going back.

Q: What was the medal of your father's that was used as a way to attack you in the press?

GORKA: This is a very important question. My father was put in prison by the Communists at the age of twenty, with a life sentence for being an anti-Communist. Prior to that, as a child, he had lived under and suffered through the fascist occupation of Hungary and had in fact protected Jewish schoolmates from abuse by the occupational German forces. As a result, his family was recognized for their support of the Jewish community in Budapest.

Once he survived the torture, the solitary confinement, and all the other aspects of being a political prisoner in a Communist dictatorship, he was liberated after six years in prison during the Hungarian Revolution of 1956 and escaped to the West with the seventeen-year-old daughter of a fellow political prisoner. They literally crawled across a minefield into Austria, and they became refugees and finally ended up in the United Kingdom, where they were married, and eventually I was born.

In the late 1970s, the dissidents, the anti-Communists who had escaped Hungary created a revitalized version of the Vitez chivalric order to recognize the courage of those who had resisted fascism and communism, and my father was awarded membership in that order in 1979. On special occasions, such as the inauguration ball, I wear that medal in memory of my parents' heroism. That medal has been used to smear me because a member of the earlier Vitez chivalric order had been connected to the fascist takeover of Hungary. It's guilt by association and ignores the fact that members of the original Vitez order have been recognized by Yad Vashem in Israel for saving members of the Jewish community in Hungary. But, again, for the media, it's not about truth. It's about narrative. It's about attacking people who are associated with President Trump. But I still have that medal, and I am proud of what it represents in terms of my parents' resistance to Nazis and Communists, and I will remain proud of it.

Q: Are there people in the Trump Administration who conspire against him?

GORKA: Well, conspiracy connotes some kind of organized group. I wouldn't go so far as to say there's evidence of that. But, I will tell you from my own experience and the experience of individuals in the Trump administration who are political appointees, yes, there are people in the administration, civil servants and political appointees, who are undermining the president and his agenda on a daily basis.

There are people from the Obama administration still in place—and that is a very serious problem. Bureaucrats who are sympathetic to the globalizing, post-modern, relativist policies and ideologies of the Left and the radical Left, are working every day to undermine the president—making it all the more remarkable that he has achieved as much as he has.

I was speaking in front of a group of leaders of conservative organizations, just after the midterm elections in 2018, and they asked me, "What should we say to the president if we see him? What's the priority?" And I was very clear with them: he needs to hire the right people; and you should advise him who those people are. I said it doesn't matter whether the most important topic to you is the Second Amendment, Freedom of Speech, Pro-Life issues, tax reform, or de-regulation—no good things will happen if you don't get the first question right, and that's the question of personnel.

There's a saying in Washington, D.C.: "Personnel is policy." Absolutely right. And this is perhaps the greatest weakness of the Trump administration. When we won the election in 2016, it was with a very small group of people who accompanied him into the White House—and many of those have since left, myself included. As an outsider, an anti-establishment candidate, President Trump did not have a long roster of likely appointees outside his selections for the courts and cabinet positions. The question of building a cadre of MAGA loyalists around the president remains a very important one and will be crucial to his second term.

Q: What was it like working with the president and what was your happiest and most memorable moment with Mr. Trump?

GORKA: It was incredible. It still sends shivers down my spine when I think about going to work on Saturday,

January 21, 2017, the day after the inauguration. Here I was, a legal immigrant to the United States, a guy with a funny accent being driven in an unmarked van from the Transition Offices to the Eisenhower Executive Office Building on the White House compound. Being given my blue badge, and then walking over to the West Wing—which was empty (I guess people were still recovering from the celebrations of the inaugural ball!)—and having the freedom, as a deputy assistant to the president for strategic issues, to wander around the corridors of the White House. It was a dream come true.

Working with President Trump was inspirational because of his will to fight and never give up. This man—who is rich beyond rich, and famous beyond famous—sacrificed his personal comfort and security to represent us, to fight the swamp creatures and the Fake News Industrial Complex. That will be a lifelong inspiration for me.

What was my proudest moment? It's interesting. There was a photograph included in my last book *Why We Fight* that may surprise some but really does represent my proudest moment. It wasn't taken when I escorted eighteen soon-to-be Green Berets to meet their new commander in chief, or the first time I met Mr. Trump, instead it was standing in the back of the Rose Garden on a beautiful late-Spring-early-Summer day as the president gave a formal press conference on his decision to remove us from the disastrous Paris Climate Accords. The climate accords weren't one of my responsibilities, but I was there because of the significance of what this act meant. It was a rejection of the Left's fake idol of environmentalism. It was about the principle that undergirded our campaign and every significant policy decision of the Trump administration, which is national sovereignty. And it was expressed perfectly when the president at that press conference said, "I was elected by the people, the citizens of Pittsburg, not the citizens of Paris." Of course he was. But the very fact that he had to say that tells you how far we had sunk as a nation. The establishment elites had come to believe that the goal was to serve interests outside of this nation. They put more emphasis on the interests of globalizing institutions, special interest groups, and multinational businesses than they do on the American family, the American worker, the American national interest. That is why we chose Donald Trump, a man who understands that the job of the United States president is to represent *Americans*. That is why that photograph is there in my book *Why We Fight*, because it was a clear expression of what we believe in, of what "Make America Great Again" is founded upon. It is founded upon the idea that our government should act in the interests of the American people.

Q: While working in the White House, did staff worry about the president's practice of early morning tweets? Or about the president abruptly changing his mind?

GORKA: Well, I didn't. I've met many people, conservatives, who have criticized the president's use of social media, and I've always said to them, "Look, this is one of the reasons he won. Without my friend Sean Hannity at FOX, without the president's Twitter account, Hillary Clinton would be president." That's just a fact. There's a reason that the president has more than sixty million followers on Twitter. The phenomenon of Fake News is absolutely real, and the president cuts through all of it; he just jumps over the endless lies of the mainstream media by using social media—whether it's at 4 a.m. or otherwise. In the case of international affairs, his style pays dividends. Look at how his very blunt language regarding the dictator of the Hermit Kingdom in North Korea brought Kim Jong-un to the negotiating table in Singapore and to the historic moment when a United States president stepped across the Korean demilitarized zone for the first time since the Korean War. So, no, there's nothing that I, or anyone else, can teach the president in terms of strategic communications.

Regarding his abrupt decision making or about-turns, that's his prerogative. When you're president, you see documents that others don't and get access to information that others don't have. And, as such, he takes decisive steps when he sees a problem that needs to be fixed—whether it's a strike against Syrian assets with cruise missiles after the Syrian government used chemical weapons against its own people or when his intelligence agencies inform him that a planned attack against Iran in retaliation for their downing one of our drones would result in the deaths of one hundred fifty civilians, and he cancels the planned action. He is the commander in chief, and we elected the president to make these decisions for us, using his best judgment with the information he's been given.

Q: Is President Trump the same in private as in public? What's he really like?

GORKA: I get asked this question perhaps more than any other. I can say that one of the reasons it was so easy for me to accept candidate Trump's offer to advise him on national security issues was that behind closed doors, he was exactly the same man as I had seen in public life. There was no public persona and then a completely different one in private. There was no façade that was taken down behind closed doors. What you see is what you get. Trump is Trump, to put it succinctly. And this was confirmed for me again in the White House.

Whether it was just the two of us behind closed doors in the Oval Office, or whether it was him in front of forty thousand people in a stadium, he is himself. The D.C. Swamp is littered with people who have a public persona that has nothing to do with who they really are in private. It is manufactured; it is artifice; it is completely fake. That is not the case with President Trump. Donald Trump is Donald Trump. If you want to know what he's really like, well, open a newspaper, switch on a television: that is

Donald Trump, and it is very refreshing, given what people are usually like in Washington.

Q: Did I sign a non-disclosure agreement with the Trump administration or the campaign?

GORKA: Absolutely. When I came onboard, when I met candidate Trump in June 2015 in Trump Tower, and he asked me to be his adviser on national security issues, I signed a non-disclosure agreement, which I have, of course, kept. Then, when I came into the administration and acquired my clearances, I signed all kinds of documents that protect the information that I was privy to in the administration. So, yes and yes, and unlike some people (like Omarosa), I actually took them seriously.

Q: When President Trump attacks the press, isn't that essentially an attack on the First Amendment?

GORKA: No, not at all, because he's just exercising his own First Amendment rights as a citizen and not taking government action. The First Amendment is very specifically about protecting American citizens' freedom of speech and religion from the restrictive power of the federal government. President Trump has done nothing to curtail our First Amendment rights. On the contrary, he has defended religious liberty far more zealously than his immediate predecessor, who actually brought a legal case against the Little Sisters of the Poor demanding that they violate their religious beliefs in order to support Obamacare; and if you look at how open and accessible and spontaneous Trump has been with the press, he stands as one of the most press-friendly presidents in history. Often, on the way to Marine One, he'll stop before getting in the helicopter and talk for more than half an hour to the press. If you compare that to President Obama, who actually fined, prosecuted, and surveilled journalists, and imprisoned journalists' sources, you couldn't have more of a contrast between two presidents.

Many people don't like what President Trump says or the way he says it, but that is an emotional response and not a curtailment of rights. As Ben Shapiro says, "Facts don't care about your feelings." If you look at the facts and compare President Obama to President Trump, you will see that it was Obama who truly and systematically curtailed First Amendment rights of religion and speech. On religion, even *National Review*, no friend of President Trump, published an article lamenting, "As writers who caution against hyperbole, we cannot help but conclude that the Obama administration was immensely hostile to religious liberty when judged against history and previous administrations."[1] As for the press, more charges were brought under the Espionage Act against journalists and their sources by Obama than by any other president.[2] President Trump is the opposite of that. His tweets might be controversial and elicit emotional responses, but the facts are that his respect of the First Amendment is paramount.

Q: Is it different being interviewed at Fox News versus other networks?

GORKA: Oh my, yes, indeed. Fox News is friendly. And Fox News wants to get to the truth. There are other networks that have that same objective. But if you compare those to the CNNs of the world, the MSNBCs, those networks for the most part, have no interest in the truth. They really are organizations that prioritize narrative over the truth, their own political agenda over the facts.

In my time at the White House, I felt this most acutely when I would go on, for example, Chris Cuomo's show, or Anderson Cooper's show, and it was just a tirade of either attacks against the president or absurd obsessions with things that really are of no consequence in the big scheme of things. One particular instance was when I was on Chris Cuomo's morning show. These interviews are normally meant to last three minutes or maybe six minutes if it's big breaking news. In this case, Chris Cuomo wanted to talk about one specific tweet of the president's, not about policy. But about a tweet. And he wouldn't stop. He kept on going back to the question of this tweet. To try and emphasize how absurd his obsession was, on camera, live from the north lawn of the White House, every couple of minutes I'd look at my watch and say, "Chris, we've now been discussing this tweet for eight minutes. Chris, we've now been discussing this tweet for eleven minutes." At the end of the interview, he'd spent an obsessive sixteen minutes on one tweet. He didn't want to debate policy. He didn't want to talk about substance. He wanted to talk about a tweet. So, yes, you'll never get Fox News airing a sixteen-minute segment about a tweet under the title "news." I was very happy to be associated with Fox News before and after my time in the White House, and it is very different from other networks. Long may it stay that way!

Q: Isn't it revealing that so many voices on Fox News are immigrants, rather than homegrown patriots, who defend America's values?

GORKA: Well, there are a lot of homegrown patriots on Fox. Sean Hannity, the first among them, but also Tucker Carlson, Ed Henry, Mark Levin, and others. But yes, it is notable that legal immigrants to America—like Dinesh D'Souza and myself—are so adamant, so vociferous in our love of all things American and the freedoms that we were provided when we came here. But this should surprise no one.

Read Tocqueville: it really does take the exterior perspective, the perspective of the individual coming from the outside to understand just how truly blessed and special a nation we are. If you didn't choose to be an American, if you were born here, it's very hard to understand at all what it takes for a Cuban to risk getting on a raft in shark-infested waters with his family, and to try to make it almost a hundred miles across the sea, across open waters, to freedom, to America. What it takes for the blind lawyer,

Chen Guangcheng in China to escape house arrest, climbing across the roofs of his neighbors shacks, and then hitchhiking and walking from his village to the capital to end up knocking on the door of the U.S. embassy to request asylum in the United States. It's very hard to appreciate all of this if you were born here. But if you want proof that American exceptionalism is a real thing, consider this: in Beijing there are embassies and consulates from more than a hundred fifty nations, but the blind lawyer who had fought for the rights of unborn babies in China didn't knock on the door of the embassy of Belgium, or Germany, or France, or Russia. He knocked on the front door of our embassy. Why? Because as President Ronald Reagan said, "We are the shining city on the hill," and that's what this nation represents to the world. Just go back and read the Declaration of Independence. Read our Constitution. Those words created a political reality that still today, more than two centuries later, causes other humans—who thirst for freedom—to risk their lives to come here. That provides a certain perspective.

Q: What is your opinion of Bill Kristol and the Never-Trumpers?

GORKA: Bill Kristol seems to have suffered some kind of psychological breakdown: a man who calls himself a "conservative" and then tells people to vote for Democrats. As he said in one tweet, "In a choice between President Trump and the Deep State, I choose the Deep State." That's either somebody who is willingly subversive of a duly elected president or who suffers from Trump Derangement Syndrome, which is the definition of a Never-Trumper. He and the Never-Trumpers have no right to call themselves "conservatives" anymore. I know that Kristol, a member of the GOP Swamp, has lost his sinecure at the *Weekly Standard*, which folded, and can't stand the fact that Donald Trump is president. But that is no excuse for the way he behaved during the 2016 presidential campaign and since. So the *Weekly Standard* is dead. Good riddance. Bill Kristol, the Never-Trump clique, and their journals are now utterly irrelevant.

Q. What is the president's office in Trump Tower like?

GORKA: The walls are lined with photographs of historic meetings, magazine covers, and other memorabilia of his life. His desk has piles of papers, but no computer, because the president prefers to read print rather than screens and make notations. Then there's the fabulous view of downtown Manhattan. And it looks very much like the office you would expect Donald Trump to have!

Q. You've expressed your love for science fiction. Which is your favorite *Star Wars* movie?

GORKA: That's a toughie. I love *The Empire Strikes Back*. It's the most epic *Star Wars* movie, and the most dramatic.

But I think in terms of changing the history of science fiction entertainment forever, it has to be the original *Star Wars* (or, as we now call it, *Star Wars, A New Hope*). George Lucas rehabilitated and revitalized the science fiction genre and redefined the standards for movie blockbusters and special effects. It's so sad that in the ensuing years he became the corporate entity that he—and his friends at Zoetrope like Francis Ford Coppola—fought against for so long. But, I guess, that can be the price of success.

Q: What do you think is the biggest threat America faces in the next twenty years?

GORKA: That's a fabulous question. When I came into the White House, I had a broad mandate to focus on national security issues and counterterrorism. In fact, Bill O'Reilly called me the president's "utility infielder on national security." And once I had the requisite clearances and started reading the classified reports, it became patently obvious to me that we can deal successfully with North Korea; that we can prevent Russia from being the destabilizing factor that it was under Obama; and that we can defeat theocratic Iran and global jihadism just as we defeated the ISIS caliphate.

The only real strategic threat we face is China. The United States and the West have facilitated this threat for more than forty years. Henry Kissinger's opening to China in the early 1970s and our support for China's World Trade

Organization membership and "Most Favored Nation" status have made a China an economic competitor that not only wishes to be a military competitor, but to displace us as the world's leading superpower. This isn't fiction. This is not classified. Any one of you, my dear readers, can go online and look up the phrase "One Belt, One Road." It is the Chinese government's plan to displace America and become a global hegemon by the 100th anniversary of the Chinese Communist Revolution in 2049. The good news is that President Trump is fully aware of this. After some classified briefings we gave him about what China is doing in America and around the world—in terms of economic espionage and economic warfare, President Trump developed the very resolute China policy that the we have today. Nevertheless, it will be a long struggle.

Q: Is the age of American supremacy over?

GORKA: Not at all. It was receding for the eight dark years of the Obama administration, which saw us "leading from behind" and thus withdrawing from international leadership. Our withdrawal created a vacuum in international affairs for others to exploit. We saw that with the rise of ISIS, Russia's invasion of Ukraine, and China remilitarizing itself. All that changed at noon on January 20, 2017.

Now you see a reassertion of America as the leading nation in the world. Under President Trump we are coming back. American leadership is back. It will take some time for us to get back to where we should be. But, if you look at the revitalization of NATO, if you look at the destruction of the physical caliphate of ISIS, the stabilizing of the Korean peninsula, American leadership works, and no matter for whom you voted, you have to ask yourself a very simple question: "What other nation would you like to have primacy in the world? Iran? Russia? China?" No other nation was founded on the principles of individual freedom and liberty, and that's why America should be in pole position always. Otherwise, the world is a very, very dangerous place. Just one data point: during the Obama administration, the number of international refugees climbed to sixty-five million. That is a historic record. Not even in 1945, after six years of global warfare and the redrawing of national borders, did the world see such a refugee crisis. That tells you how dangerous the world is when America recedes from its rightful and correct place as a global actor.

Q: Two and a half years into the administration, President Trump has not nominated ambassadors to key countries. What does this say about his foreign policy priorities?

GORKA: Well, in fact, that's not true. He has nominated ambassadors for all our most important embassies. The issue isn't nominations, the issue is getting the nominees approved in the face of Democrat intransigence. My favorite example is my good friend Richard Grenell, the highest-ranking openly gay official in the Trump administration, our ambassador to Germany, whose confirmation was blocked for months by Democrat Senator Charles Schumer for no good reason. The Democrats have used every trick in the book to delay almost one hundred key appointments, and to undermine others simply out of spite. The good news is that after the midterm elections in 2018, we are stronger in the Senate, despite having lost the House. So, at least when it comes to approval of nominees, it should be much smoother. But, again, don't believe everything you read in the Fake News. If you really want to know what's going on in the Swamp, you need other sources of information, like Fox News and *AMERICA First*.

Q: What should America's Russia policy be?

GORKA: When people want to understand the president's Russia policy, I always point them to the last press conference that he gave at Trump Tower before moving into the White House, the one where he handed over his companies to his children. After the press conference had ended, the president-elect was leaving the podium, and a journalist shouted something to the effect of, "What about Russia? What about Putin?" And the president stopped and gave a very succinct response that really says everything you need to know about our Russia policy, then, now, and in the future. He said, and I paraphrase here: "In theory, I would like to have good relations with Russia. Right now, it doesn't look very likely. And, if that is the case, so be it."

Now, think about that for a moment.

First part: "I would like to have better relations with Russia." Well, that's just a sound geopolitical objective. Russia is a nuclear power, with eleven time zones, that sits on the UN security council with veto power. As such, we have to strive for some kind of functioning relationship with Russia, if possible, whoever its president is.

And as to the second part: "Right now, it doesn't seem likely." That is a very apt description of Russia's relations with America. Russia under Putin is an anti-status quo actor. The Russian government destabilizes parts of the world in order to exploit that destabilization for its own interests—not as a nation, but in the interests of Putin and his *siloviki*, the Russian military-intelligence clique of former KGB officers and corrupt businessmen who really run Russia for Putin. Whether that destabilization occurs in Europe, with the invasion of Ukraine, or in the Middle East with assets deployed to Syria or elsewhere, the Russian government is not interested in strengthening the international system or normalizing representative democracy and free markets. It is an oligarchy mixed with a kleptocracy, run by a former KGB colonel. So, right now, it doesn't seem likely that the United States and Russia will have cordial relations.

Then, Donald Trump closed by saying, "So be it!" That's President Trump. He's a pragmatist—an incredibly successful businessman who looks at the world as it is, not as he would like it to be.

The reverse of that was the last administration when President Obama sent Secretary of State Hillary Clinton to meet with Foreign Secretary Sergei Lavrov of the Russian Federation to present him with a mistranslated, cheesy plastic "reset" button, in the hopes of resetting the relations between the two countries—only to have Russia exploit Obama's naïveté and incompetence by invading Ukraine.

Our policy now is that it would be good to have better relations with Russia, but since Russia is not interested, so be it. With our actions in Syria, our deployment of anti-tank missiles to Ukraine, the president's plan to deploy more U.S. troops to Poland, the initiation of stringent sanctions against the Russian regime and more,[3] the Trump administration has been tougher on Moscow than any administration since Ronald Reagan's.

Q: Do you stand with President Trump or Pope Francis on the morality of a border wall between the United States and Mexico?

GORKA: I'm a Catholic, so I recognize pontifical authority, but I would also like to inject some factual context. The Vatican is a walled city. It has a massive wall around it. The idea that walls by themselves are immoral is plainly absurd. People lock their door at night; nations have borders; civilized communities, since the most ancient of times, have built walls. Why? Because you wish to protect that which is inside. You close your front door and lock it at night, not because you hate everybody outside, but because you love that which is inside your home, and you wish to protect it. Our borders are the doors into our country. And the idea that you do not police who comes into your home, or your nation, is suicidal.

Here is something that should make all people—all Americans, liberals included—want to support the president and his building of the wall: I am a legal immigrant to the United States of America. The first lady is a legal immigrant to the United States. Legal immigration is fine. But it is terribly immoral to encourage illegal immigrants to put their lives and their children's lives into the hands of human traffickers who take their orders from drug cartels, rape women, and don't care if the immigrants die after they have paid for their passage.

And then there is the domestic economic aspect. Every illegal alien who comes across the border, who is prepared to work illegally for cash, undermines the capacity of working-class Americans—including working-class immigrants who have come here lawfully—to provide for themselves and their families.

So, whether you're Pope Francis or Nancy Pelosi, if you really care about immigrants and the poor, then you should support the building of a border wall and the enforcement of our border laws. National sovereignty is a good thing. Without national sovereignty you don't have a nation. That is the underlying philosophy of Donald Trump's trade and international policies, and it is grounded in a very defensible morality.

Q: What is your take on Mohammed Bin Salman, the man who is effectively running Saudi Arabia; is he good, bad, or crazy?

GORKA: I don't know if he's crazy. I'm not a mental health professional. Is he good or bad? When I was in the White House, we worked very, very diligently to try and change Saudi Arabia's behavior when it came to the sponsorship of bad actors and the propagation of jihadi ideology across the world. For far too many decades, members of the royal family and the ruling elite were on the wrong side of the war against global jihadism, and if you want to be an ally of America, or if you want to be a partner, that attitude cannot be maintained.

We made it clear to Riyadh, and to Mohammad Bin Salman, that they had to undertake what in the White House we called, "behavior modification." And, they did. In May 2017 President Trump gave a speech at the American Islamic Arab Summit in Riyadh.[4] Speaking to the fifty-two Muslim and Arab heads of state sitting in front of him, he called on the Muslim leaders to rid their countries and houses of worship of terrorists and radicals. Within two weeks of that speech, the nations of the Gulf Cooperation Council—Saudi Arabia included—announced they were boycotting and terminating diplomatic relations with Qatar, which was one of the worst perpetrators of financing jihadism around the world. That is behavior modification.

Since that time, Mohammad Bin Salman has initiated other reforms in Saudi Arabia, but it has been a rocky road, especially after the murder of Saudi dissident Jamal Khashoggi—a murder that has been indecently exploited by the press as yet another means to attack President Trump for his diplomatic efforts with the Kingdom. Of course, Khashoggi didn't deserve to be murdered, but the press has made him out to be a liberal martyr, which is not true. The idea that an admitted member of the Muslim Brotherhood, a close associate of Osama Bin Laden, and an advocate for Islamist theocracy, all of which Khashoggi was, is somehow a freedom fighter for democracy tells you everything you need to know about the moral and professional bankruptcy of today's media.

Q: Would you have authorized the air strikes in Syria after the Syrian regime gassed its own citizens?

GORKA: Absolutely. I can't go into details, but I saw the intelligence at the time. The President took action to send a very clear message, not just to Syria's President Bashar al-Assad, but to Assad's sponsors, and to other bad actors around the world, that America will act against those who think they can use forbidden weapons of war against unarmed women and children. So, yes, absolutely, I'd have had no problem in launching cruise missiles against Assad as the president did.

Q: What is the threat of Islamic fundamentalism to the United States and the world community now and in the future?

GORKA: It remains. ISIS's physical caliphate has been destroyed thanks to the leadership and policy decisions of President Trump. But ISIS itself, as an organization, has not been destroyed; it has moved into other areas. It has even established facilities in Afghanistan. Al Qaeda is not dead either. Al Qaeda is still active, especially in Africa and southern Asia.

Right now the threat is contained. The key metric for how effectively it will remain contained will be a function of how well we help our Muslim partners—especially Jordan, Egypt, and Saudi Arabia—and regional powers like Israel, to deal with the threat. Right now, the president has reshaped the geostrategic reality in the Middle East in ways that make a lasting containment possible—from destroying the ISIS caliphate, to dramatically improving relations with Israel, to seeking realistic diplomatic solutions with the Arab world—and that will continue for as long as Donald Trump is president.

Q: Aside from Islamic fundamentalism what, in your opinion, is America's greatest, non-state actor threat?

GORKA: I don't believe that any non-state actor poses a threat the way China does. I also don't subscribe to the theory that the most serious sub-state or non-state actor threat comes from hackers in the cyber domain, as many do. For a cyber threat to be significant to America, it really has to be of a nation-state-sponsored variety, such as China and Russia. Hackers can do damage to an individual or an organization, but not at a strategic level. Unless you are a state actor, you cannot wage war using cyber tools. So, not cyber.

Really, it's criminal cartels, it's transnational organized crime. If you look at what's happening on the southern border, if you look at what's happening in Mexico where tens of thousands of people have been killed in recent years, if you look at the tragedy of human-trafficking, it is the drug cartels that are the top non-state actor threat after the global jihadi movement.

Q: We have seen liberal media bias for years; do you think that will ever improve?

GORKA: I'm often asked about media bias, and my dispassionate response is, "Describe to me the scenarios under which it would improve." There are two likely options. Number one, the so-called mainstream media have some kind of epiphany: they look in the mirror one day and decide that they're going to be fair, to suddenly become apolitical. But why would they do that?

Despite having so many of their stories against the Trump administration proved false, the media have not lessened their attacks; if anything, the lies, the vituperation, and perfidious mendacity have increased. So, no it's highly unlikely that the media will suddenly develop a conscience and become apolitical.

The second scenario is that market forces will prevail and that the news media will reform because it is in their economic interest. Well, you would think so. But will they?

CNN on a good night has around 600,000 viewers. That's less than half a percent of the U.S. population. So why does CNN still function? Well, because the market is rigged. CNN is routinely bundled on cable packages, so CNN does not have to satisfy market forces. People don't have to pay for CNN; they get CNN automatically when they order essentially any cable package. That is why Social Media is all the more important, and why everyone—and I mean everyone—who believes in the Make America Great Again agenda must be on Twitter, Facebook, and Instagram, supporting the president, calling out the lies of the media and highlighting the corruption of the Democrats.

Q: From your perspective, as a son of refugees from a totalitarian society, can you comment on the intolerance of free speech exhibited by many on the American Left?

GORKA: It's absolutely stunning. There's a reason that the First Amendment is about freedom of speech and religion.

There's a reason that the Second Amendment is about the right to keep and bear arms. These are fundamental. They are connected at the hip: the capacity to protect your freedom and the capacity to express your freedom.

The Left is only tolerant insofar as you agree with their views. In the now famous words of U.S. soccer player Megan Rapinoe, she (and other Leftists) are happy to have "a real, substantive conversation" with anyone who "believes in the same things we believe in."[5] As for anyone else, they are bigots, of course. A patriot like John F. Kennedy would not be allowed in the Democrat party of today. Instead, he would be labeled a fascist for his anti-Communist, pro-national security stances. How did this happen?

I think in many cases this is a natural function of how Leftist philosophy is built on the idea of "collectivism"— that is, favoring the group over the individual—and "statism," giving power to the state. Conservatives, people on the political Right, focus on the God-given rights of the individual. On the Left, they focus on favored groups— Communists, National Socialists, the various self-declared "identity politics" or "victim" groups today in the West— whose collective interests outweigh individual rights (including the natural rights guaranteed us by the Constitution).

In all sincerity, all politics boils down to one question: do you believe man is perfectable, and therefore do you believe in social engineering? The Right says, no, man is fallen and cannot be made "perfect," however you define that. "Conservatism" comes from this realistic vision and a desire to "conserve" traditions that have proven their worth. The Left believes the opposite—that man is like putty, infinitely malleable, and can be reconfigured into *homo Sovieticus* if you're in the USSR, or into an androgynous, socialist snowflake if you're in the West today. Only one of these views is supported by the last six thousand years of human history that we have available to us, and it's stunning that so few people have learned the lesson of recent millennia: not only is man limited in his capacity to shape and engineer his fellow man, but when he tries to do so, intolerance, tyranny, oppression, and even genocide are the results.

Q: Will we ever see Hillary Clinton behind bars?

GORKA: I don't know. I think people around her may see jailtime or be prosecuted. I think people in the DOJ and FBI of the Obama administration—such as Andrew McCabe—who are clearly corrupt, will face federal charges now that William Barr is the attorney general. I dearly hope that Lady Justice is blind. I try not to make predictions, but the idea that your last name will protect you from prosecution is fundamentally un-American.

Q: How do we heal the hate that supporters of the Left have for supporters of the Right?

GORKA: That's a topic for a Ph.D. dissertation!

I've said it before, and I'll say it again: the Left is fueled today by hate, while our fuel on the Right is love, love of country.

Take Michelle Obama, who actually said that the first time she was ever proud of her country was when Democrats started rallying around her husband in the primaries in 2008.[6] What does that tell you about a person's perspective on America?

There is a reason that the Left has become so aggressive and destructive. It is because they truly believe that the ends justify the means; and since they believe they can make the perfect society, then all means are justified to achieve that goal. And, as such, they will hate you if you stand against them. So, what do we do about it?

I don't think there is much we can do for the most hard-bitten of our adversaries in the political sphere. It's very hard to imagine an Alexandria Ocasio-Cortez or a Charles Schumer being respectful in a debate. Just look at the video of Schumer and Nancy Pelosi in the Oval Office with the President before the government shutdown at the end of 2018. Charles Schumer doesn't even make eye contact with the president. He is disdainful of his interlocutor. That tells you everything you need to know. Ask yourself, when do you stop hating someone? The answer is when you have enough self-awareness to know that it's wrong. I don't expect to see that from the key figures on the Left.

Many who have been indoctrinated by the Left don't want to engage in dialogue because they have no ideas that stand up to scrutiny. Look at the videos of my friend, Austin Fletcher, who goes by "Fleccas" on YouTube. When he goes with a camera and a microphone to the demonstrations of the radical Left, if you look at the young people, their indoctrination is very, very shallow. After two or three questions posed by Austin, these young Leftists have nothing left. They have no argument. They have no facts. It's just slogans about "Trump is a Nazi," and those who vote for him are "racists." With people who are literally brainwashed, you deal with their hatred by using what the Left so effectively exploits: emotion. It's not facts that will bring them around. It's emotions, sadly.

Look at the argument over the border wall. The conservative argument is most often about facts and constitutional first principles: it has to do with arrest rates on the border, the crime rates of illegal immigrants, drug flows, the importance of enforcing our existing laws, the necessity of defending our national sovereignty, and so on. My approach is different. Use the empathetic argument. For example, if you tell a protester against our immigration laws, or somebody who doesn't want the wall that 60 to 80 percent of the women smuggled by human traffickers across Mexico to our border are raped along the way[7]—that resonates emotionally. Or tell them this: of the twelve thousand illegal immigrant children being cared for by the HHS in June 2018, ten thousand came here unaccompanied by their parents.[8] Their parents had given the children to human smugglers—to agents of the drug cartels—to bring them here. By encouraging illegal immigration, the Left is encouraging this sort of endangerment of children. Then, your argument is a very simple one: Do you care for those young women? Do you care for those children? If you want to protect those young women, if you want to protect the young children of Latin America or South America, then we must build the wall that will be the only thing that discourages people from taking these horrible risks. That's not a cold, factual response. It is one that appeals to the heart, to the soul, and that is still true, and that is one way to undermine the hate.

Q: How much of a problem is the indoctrination that happens on college campuses today?

GORKA: We have ceded education to the radical Left. The idea today that we have "safe spaces" on university campuses, that we have "Free Speech Zones," when in fact the Free Speech Zone in America should extend from the Canadian border to the Mexican border, and from the Atlantic Seaboard to the Pacific, tells you how things have changed. Berkeley, which prides itself on being the home of the Free Speech Movement is now no longer interested in protecting anybody's free speech if they are not left-wing, if they are not a radical Leftist.

Look at the experience of individuals like Ben Shapiro, who either are disinvited from speaking at college campuses, or are burdened with such absurd security costs that it makes it almost impossible for a group to finance an event.

Here we have the fruits grown from the seeds of the radical Left of the 1960s. First they tried to ignite in America the kind of violent Marxist overthrow that was attempted on the streets of Paris in 1968, but it failed. They very soon realized that in America, given our unique historic development, our rugged individualism, our individual liberty, and our freedom of speech and religion, this use of Marxist or Maoist tactics would not function in a country like ours. These individuals—some of whom were terrorists, such as Bernardine Dohrn and Bill Ayers, members of the Weathermen Underground— didn't retire. They didn't surrender their objective to turn America into some kind of radical Leftist construct when their "Days of Rage" failed in 1969. Instead, they became educators. They became high school teachers. In some cases, like with Ayers and Dohrn, they became tenured professors at otherwise reputable colleges. Why? Because they knew their Trotsky, they knew their Lenin—in fact, they knew what Hitler had taught his acolytes: "If you give me their children, I will control their future." So they took the indoctrination from the streets into the classrooms. And that is how today we have courses upon courses that have nothing to do with our heritage, with our Judeo-Christian culture, with patriotic American history, with the wisdom of the Founding

Fathers. Instead, every college that has federal funding for deans of diversity, courses on gender studies, on so-called "Critical Studies" which is really the criticism of all that is Western and good. They've created generations obsessed with environmentalism, which is the god of the atheist Left. We have arrived at the point where you can major in English at otherwise serious universities without ever having studied Shakespeare. This is what the conservative surrendering of education has wrought in America.

There were responses, there were resistance movements in the form of the homeschooling movement and amazing institutions like Hillsdale College that do not accept federal funding and therefore have managed to maintain an independent stance that allows them to focus on the truth and teach the founding principles of our Republic and our civilization.

Part of the problem in higher education is tenure. The tenure track system encourages group-think, encourages the hiring, promotion, and finally lifetime appointment of individuals who agree with the radical Leftist agenda.

The good news is that now we have other movements. Turning Point USA is a superb response to the indoctrination that goes on in higher education, and Charlie Kirk, who runs it, has done wonderful things in just a few years to push back the insanity on campus. Campus Reform and others, including individuals like Steven Crowder, are taking the principles of the Founding to campuses. But this will be a very, very long project. It will take at least two generations to get us back to the point where colleges are about challenging thought not about funneling thought into one politically approved agenda.

Q: Have you considered running for office?

GORKA: People have said I should run for president, and I thank them for the compliment, but I can't because I wasn't born here! I have toyed with the idea of running for office in Virginia, but I'm having too much fun on my radio show and, I think, doing some good without having to become a political Swamp dweller.

Q: What's in store after 2024?

GORKA: What's in store for 2024? That could be the subject for my next book!

Q: Is President Trump's impact here to stay?

GORKA: There are very few people like Trump out there, but I think that he has changed American politics in ways that are irrevocable. Politics as usual cannot continue in exactly the same way as it did before.

If you look just at the way messaging works, his use of social media, Twitter, how certain interests—the Never-Trumpers—have been totally broken. I don't know if you'll see a lot more Trumps—I don't know that they exist!—but we will certainly see more celebrities and non-politicians running for office.

Trump shredded the rulebook for running a campaign. If you look at how he campaigned—where he won, how he crossed over into Democrat party strongholds, working-class areas, and even beat Mitt Romney among minority voters as a Republican presidential candidate[9]—that "blue collar conservative"[10] Trump Effect has changed American politics in ways that will endure. His presidency is clearly already historic.

Q: What is your favorite, most important American value?

GORKA: That's so difficult to choose. But, really, I think it's common sense, which might not exist in crazy, urban areas like Washington, D.C. But if you get out of the groupthink areas and into the areas that are derisively called "flyover states," the people there are full of common sense. I haven't seen it exist at such a level anywhere around the world—and I have seen a lot of the world, from Europe to Asia to Africa. Americans are uniquely pragmatic—in a good way. When something is broken, they fix it. They don't sit down and have a nice cappuccino with biscotti and discuss the various ways to fix it. They actually do it. They don't have arguments about who should fix it, or why we should fix it. They just fix it. So, common sense allied with a can-do attitude—that really is very, very American.

Q: What can the local citizen or community do to support President Trump's work to Make America Great Again?

GORKA: That's such an important question. Everyone, everybody, has a role to play in Making America Great Again—and Keeping America Great. And the easiest way to do so, the most obvious way, is to support local candidates and elections with your time and your money, supporting those who share an agenda that is about eternal principles, eternal truths, getting America back to where it should be in the world.

But, beyond that, everyone should take an active role in representing those values on social media. Conservatives are occasionally "throttled" or censored on platforms like Twitter and Facebook, but that only makes it all the more important to be active, to re-tweet the president's announcements, to call out lies that you see in the media, and to campaign for conservative ideas everywhere from the local school board, to the city council, to the county level, to the state level. American citizens have always taken an active interest in politics at all levels since the inception of our country—and it has never been more important than now. Social media is the pamphlet of the 18th century. Don't just complain. Don't be shy. Don't think, "Oh, I can't make a difference." Every individual makes a difference. Get an account on Twitter. Get an account on Facebook. However old you are, however much of a technological klutz you may think you are, stand up for the truth because the stakes couldn't be higher.

When we see that the Victims of Communism Memorial Foundation publishes its annual survey last year, and they find that 52 percent of American millennials would like to live in a Socialist or Communist country, then you have a responsibility to help us push back on that shocking and dreadful reality. After the ideology of Karl Marx took the lives of more than one hundred million people in the last century, what are you prepared to do to make sure that doesn't happen here in America? The least you can do is tell the truth about what socialism does to a country, to any nation where it has been tried. Since Karl Marx wrote *Das Kapital* in 1867, forty countries have tried communism—and the result has always been economic, social, and human catastrophe. So, support the MAGA agenda by being a representative of it in everything you say and do. Don't get unnecessarily preachy about it. But tell the truth and be part of the solution, not the problem. That's the Trump Way!

Q: What is your advice for conservatives living in such Democrat strongholds as California and Massachusetts?

GORKA: Never give up. Look at what we achieved in areas we were told would never vote Republican again. I traveled with the president to Youngstown, Ohio, to a rally in July 2017, and it was remarkable. We landed at

a base, got into a convoy, drove a few miles to the stadium, and on the left-hand side of the road all we saw
was broken-down steel mill after broken-down steel
mill. On the right-hand side, for miles all we saw were
Americans wearing their MAGA hats, waving the American flag. We got to the stadium, and then I saw the
power of MAGA and the Trump Effect. These people
were clearly manual laborers, salt-of-the-earth, true
Americans who had been registered Democrats. Their
parents and grandparents had been Democrats—blue-
collar Democrats—but when the first lady and the president came out on the stage, he couldn't start his speech
for minutes because they were chanting, "USA! USA!
Drain the swamp!" That's incredible. That's a billionaire, Republican president in Steel Valley, Ohio. If it can
happen there, then don't give up anywhere—even in San
Francisco or Boston. Yes, parts of California and Massachusetts seem to have lost their minds in terms of how
they reelect people who want to bankrupt their communities and create conditions that are unlivable. But if
the president can win over a Democrat county like
Trumbull County, which hasn't been won by a non-
incumbent Republican since 1928,[11] and almost win
Mahoning County, which two counties divide
Youngstown, Ohio, between them, then truly anything
is possible. So, hold the line, never give up, keep the
faith, and just remember we owe it to the president. He

has sacrificed everything for us, so the least we can do is to support him.

AN EXCLUSIVE INTERVIEW WITH PRESIDENT DONALD TRUMP

APRIL 23, 2019, OVAL OFFICE, THE WHITE HOUSE

GORKA: As the child of parents who escaped Communism, I was very moved when you told Congress that America would never be a Socialist country. Did you ever think that any American president would have to say such a thing to Congress?

TRUMP: No, I never did. I never thought it would be part of the dialogue. I am happy to report that I don't think that it will be lasting very long. Our country is doing better than it has ever done economically, with the stock market and 401Ks—and I'm not just talking about people of wealth, I'm talking about people who haven't had a job in years and now have jobs. We have the greatest number of jobs that we've ever had, almost one hundred sixty million, the stock market today just hit another all-time high—all three markets—and people are great. So I think that it would be very surprising to me if that debate carries forward much longer. I hope it won't, but it could very well be a big dialogue, a big part of the election, but we're talking about not so very far away. Can you imagine that Sebastian, like seventeen months? Can you imagine that? Time flies!

GORKA: It does!

TRUMP: Amazing

GORKA: Back when I served as your deputy assistant for strategy…

TRUMP: And did a great job. You really did a great job!

GORKA: Thank you. In this room, it was just the two of us, May or June of 2017. You said to me, "Sebastian, they'll never find anything because there isn't anything," in regard to Russian collusion.

TRUMP: It's true.

GORKA: Since then, you have been vindicated by Congress, twice, and now by the Department of Justice with the close of the Mueller investigation. Yet on the Left, many still refuse to give up their Russian delusions. Presumably, this is a positive factor for you in 2020 and for the broader Make America Great Again agenda. Is it good that they're constantly beating this dead horse? Is it a good thing for you, Mr. President?

TRUMP: Look, it was so preposterous that at the beginning, I didn't even take it seriously. When I first heard about "Russia and the Trump administration," I literally didn't even take it seriously, but then I saw that they'll do anything to win. They'll say anything they have to say. And if you had told me that it could lead to a special counsel, with all that that entails, I would have said, "That's an impossibility." But we won, there was no collusion. The problem is I think they could have made that determination in the first two days. I also think that a special counsel never should have been appointed. It's disgraceful for our country. But we handled it properly. I gave a level of transparency that's never been given in the history of our country before, ever. And I did that for a reason. I did that: number one, I thought it was important, and number two, I knew there was nothing there.

GORKA: This is something that I had to get used to when I came to work for you. As an incredibly successful businessman, as a billionaire who had relations, good relations, with the media for decades, were you prepared for what

happened when you became president, and how the media
has treated you, treated you and your family and anybody
who works for you?

TRUMP: Well I don't think anybody can be prepared to
take the greatest onslaught in the history of politics by a
very dishonest media. It was really incredible. And you
know, the amazing thing is that we're doing great with poll
numbers. In fact, I see, we're at forty-nine today in Rasmus-
sen… we're at fifty-one in another one. And that's with an
onslaught that nobody's ever seen before; it's amazing. And
so I think that the word "prepared" means that you have
to prepare yourself quickly, and I prepared myself quickly.
It's incredible that the public gets it, they really get it. And
if you look at the approval rating of the press, it's unbeliev-
ably low, lower than it's ever been. And it should be. You
know the incredible thing: I'll explain it to the public, and
they get it better than anyone. But I will have a story, and
the press will take that story, and if it's good they'll make
it bad, or they'll make it as little good as possible. And it's
incredible to watch, because they don't really know the
story, and they don't know the inner workings of the story.
I'm not talking about all media, but I'm talking about a
hell of a lot of it; it is totally dishonest, it's incredible.

 For instance, you'll see stories on Sean Hannity, or
Laura Ingraham, or Tucker Carlson, or Lou Dobbs, or *Fox
and Friends* in the morning, revealing a major scandal
[committed by liberals], and it won't be picked up by one

paper. It is really incredible. I call it suppression, because they suppress all this news. You would think their ambition would outweigh whatever it is that they're doing because they'd all get Pulitzer prizes. Instead they get Pulitzer prizes for telling lies.

GORKA: When I was last here to see you, I was in the White House Press Briefing Room, and Abilio "Jim" Acosta bowls past me, grabs my shoulder, and in front of witnesses, says "What are you doing here? This is for real journalists." That's what Acosta said. He has a high opinion of himself.

TRUMP: You know, it is incredible how wrong they have been.

GORKA: And the Mueller report ...

TRUMP: Mueller would have loved to have written something negative, Mueller and his Trump-haters, angry Democrats. If they had one phone call, if they had anything, even a small conversation, they would've tried to make it into a collusion. They spent thirty-five million dollars, and at the end of two years, they say there's no collusion.

GORKA: According to the Heritage Foundation, your first year in office was even more successful than Ronald Reagan's.[1] By any objective measure, your administration in the first two years has achieved more than any modern administration in eight years. Are the next six years of your presidency going to be enough to undo all the harm inflicted by Obama and Clinton?

TRUMP: Well I think we've done a lot of it in the first two years despite the phony witch hunt. I think that I've done more than any president in the first two years. I wrote out a list for you. It's point after point after point.[2]

GORKA: Great. Thank you, sir.

TRUMP: These are just things that we've done, all big things. And today, again, we hit the highest ever on the Nasdaq and S&P.

GORKA: What did Paul Krugman say after your election? That the stock market would crash and never recover?[3]

TRUMP: Oh, is that what he said?

GORKA: He said never recover.

TRUMP: Boy, I'll tell you, if you listened to him… and the guy probably gets a big medal.

GORKA: They gave him the Nobel prize.

TRUMP: For nothing!

GORKA: In the last two years, if you look at Capitol Hill, it's been a handful of people who've had your back. It would seem a no-brainer for the GOP to look at what you've achieved and hitch their wagon to your agenda. Does the establishment on the Right understand the significance of 2016, and is that going to change, do you think?

TRUMP: I've had great support from a larger number of Republicans than people would think.

GORKA: Really?

TRUMP: Yeah. I really have had.

GORKA: But quietly, you mean.

TRUMP: Yes. But I've been disappointed by some, and some are just openly, you know, out there—I mean, they just don't vote for anything that we're doing. I don't have to say who because all you have to do is check the votes. It's pretty shocking. But I think I've had a lot more support from Republican congressmen and Republican senators than people think. I really do. I think I've had some really good support. I've also supported them. One of the greatest moments is the election of 2018. We won.

GORKA: Right. They were great results.

TRUMP: We won. We picked up two seats in the Senate, and I got rid of two senators that, frankly, had been very bad to me. They were hostile to me. They're gone. We're at fifty-three. Big difference between fifty-three and fifty-one. So, we won. Judges, remember, are confirmed by the Senate. Now, did we lose the House? Yeah, but I couldn't campaign for all of the people. You know, it's just so many. I campaigned for Senate, and look at the seats we picked up, with Josh Hawley, with so many, you look at Indiana, you look at North Dakota.

Look at the seats we picked up, brand new seats. I was told that Heidi Heitkamp in North Dakota could not be beaten, you would be wasting your time. And Kevin Cramer ran a great race in North Dakota; he had great support for me.

I was told that it was going to be very hard to win in Missouri; it was going to be very hard to win in Indiana. We won in Missouri; we won in Indiana. In Tennessee, look how great Republican Marsha Blackburn did.

How about Florida? You look at Florida, the Senate race between Republican Rick Scott and Democrat Ron DeSantis. We won. Look at the governor of Georgia, where Oprah, President Obama, and Mrs. Obama campaigned; they staked out there and they campaigned. I went there for Brian Kemp, and we won. Look at Ohio, the governor of Ohio, how important is Ohio? The governor's great. But he was down 7 and he ended up winning by 7 after that final campaign stop, last day, took him up 14 points. Andy Barr in Kentucky was down by 7; he won by 6. Oh also, Cindy Hyde-Smith in the Senate, she was down by 3 or 4 points, and I went down and did two rallies. These aren't speeches, these are rallies—big deals, with twenty or twenty-five thousand people, or more....

GORKA: I remember when you were with Corey Lewandowski, and we'd always have to expand the stadium. You'd have one location, it wouldn't be big enough. We'd have to find another one, we'd have to find another one....

TRUMP: Sebastian, I've never had an empty seat.

GORKA: And they're always waiting outside, thousands outside.

TRUMP: Tens of thousands waiting for hours. It shows you how unfair the press is. I go to El Paso, and Beto O'Rouke at that time was the hot new thing, and he heard I was going to do a rally. So he called for a rally. He had 502 people show up. I had 12,000 inside and 35,000 outside. And I mean that place was popping; it broke the [attendance] record [for the site]. We had big screens. And the press said we both had "large" rallies. One reporter in the *New York Times* actually said his rally was larger than mine....

GORKA: Fake News. In the last year, the tactics of the media and the Left have been literally disgraceful. From Justice Kavanaugh, his treatment, to the Covington School boys. Do you expect the tactics to get even worse before 2020? If so, what should the average American do?

TRUMP: I don't think they can get worse. Because I've been a student of politics for a long time. In the history of politics, I don't think I've ever seen anything like Judge Kavanaugh. Those were fabricated stories, fabricated stories. And I have never seen anyone treated so badly as him, in front of his wife and his children, great people. Never saw anything like it. I don't think it can get worse than that; it can only be the same. That's the highest standard there is in town.

And will it continue? The *New York Times* basically has given up journalistic standards. They've said, "We don't care; we'll say anything." Essentially, they're just making up stories. They don't even call for confirmation; they don't call for quotes. If they're doing a bad story on me, they don't call for a response. And they couldn't care less. If we tell them it's untrue, it makes zero difference to them, zero.

GORKA: As a result, how important is social media?

TRUMP: Without it, I guess, I wouldn't have a voice. Even other voices would be drowned out, you know like Sean

Hannity and Lou Dobbs, and *Fox and Friends* in the morning, other people like Steve Doocy and Ainsley Earhardt, and the whole group, you know, great people. But I think they're drowned out because eventually they have to succumb to this horror show that's going on right now. "Fake News" is a great term for it. I hope I get credit for coming up with that one. But now the Fake News uses it all the time, they'll say "Fake News has reported," they'll say it like they're legitimate, like they're talking about somebody else....

I never thought the press could be so dishonest. The Democrat party, the radical, liberal Democrats, are in absolute partnership with the media. It's crazy.

And when you think of what I've done.

I've strengthened the military to a point where it's never been. The military was so depleted, we were close to not having a military.

I've rebuilt the steel industry; steel is hopping now. We were not going to have steel made in this country.

Energy, look, we're now the number one energy producer in the world, oil and gas. We weren't close when I got elected. I'm approving pipelines now at a pace that nobody's ever even thought possible. They need them desperately in Texas. I approved all of them: the Dakota Access, the Keystone. I approved them immediately. I got ANWR in Alaska. Ronald Reagan—and everybody who's tried since—was unable to get that, and I got that approved in Alaska.

Look at the judges. I'm now over one hundred twenty judges, two of whom are Supreme Court justices.

GORKA: Do you think you'll get a third Supreme Court justice?

TRUMP: That I don't know. I hope she [Ruth Bader Ginsburg] and everybody else lives for a long time.

GORKA: Last two questions. How are we doing, Mr. President, in defeating the Deep State?

TRUMP: Well, I think, if it all works out, I will consider it one of the greatest things I've done. You look at what's happened to the absolute scum at the top of the FBI. You look at what's happening over at the Justice Department, now we have a great attorney general. Whereas before that, with Jeff Sessions, it was a disaster. Just a total disaster. He was an embarrassment to the great state of Alabama. And I put him there because he endorsed me, and he wanted it so badly. And I wish he'd never endorsed me. It would have been the greatest non-endorsement I ever had. But it's too bad. But now we have a great attorney general. And I think with the destruction of the Deep State, certainly I've done big damage. They've come after me in so many different ways; it's been such a disgrace. But I think it'll be one of my great achievements.

GORKA: Okay, last question. What would President Trump of 2019 have said to candidate Trump in 2015, by way of advice?

TRUMP: Always be prepared for the unexpected.

DIRECT FROM PRESIDENT TRUMP: DEBATE PREP TO WIN THE BIG ARGUMENT

O n April 23, 2019, I visited President Trump in the Oval Office to interview him for this book. He gave me this document to show all the good news that the Fake News Industrial Complex is keeping from the American people.

This list of what President Donald Trump achieved in just two years would be an incredible collection of achievements for a *two-term* president.

These conservative victories have enraged the Left, which is now more radical than ever, making the 2020 election even more important than the history-making 2016 election.

Use this incredible list of achievements with your friends and anyone who is undecided—and remind them of the stakes involved and the threat the Left poses.

TRUMP ADMINISTRATION ACCOMPLISHMENTS

- 5.5 million jobs created since my election, with 196,000 jobs added last month
- More Americans are working today than ever before in our history – nearly 160 million Americans now have jobs
- March 2019 was the 102nd straight month of positive job growth; longest streak ever
- There are a record number of job openings
- A record 73 percent of newly employed workers were people who were out of the workforce and are now coming off the sidelines and into the workforce
- The unemployment rate has remained at or below 4 percent for 13 straight months—it recently reached its lowest rate in nearly FIFTY YEARS
- We have created half a million manufacturing jobs since my election—more manufacturing jobs were created in 2018 than any single year in the last 20 years
- Blue-collar jobs recently grew at the fastest rate in more than THREE DECADES
- GDP grew at 3 percent during the four quarters of 2018, the fastest rate of any calendar year since 2005

- Wages grew by 3.2 percent over the past 12 months, the largest increase in 10 years; wage growth in 2018 was fastest for the lowest wage earners
- Hispanic-American unemployment in February fell to its lowest rate in history
- African-American and Asian-American unemployment rates have reached all-time record lows
- Women's unemployment is at its lowest rate in 65 years
- Veteran unemployment has reached the lowest rate in nearly 20 years
- Youth unemployment reached the lowest rate in nearly half a century
- Unemployment rate for Americans without a high school diploma hit a new low
- Unemployment rate for disabled Americans recently hit a record low
- Over 5 million Americans have been lifted off food stamps since the election
- Median income for Hispanic-Americans surpassed $50,000 for the first time ever
- Home-ownership among Hispanics recently hit the highest rate in nearly a decade
- The official poverty rates for African-Americans and Hispanic-Americans have reached their lowest levels ever recorded
- Manufacturing, consumer, and small business confidence recently set record highs

- A recent study found that 8 in 10 businesses plan to hire more workers this year
- Signed the biggest package of tax cuts and reforms in history; since then, almost $600 billion dollars poured back into the U.S., and more than 6 million workers received new bonuses, better jobs, and bigger paychecks
- Saved Family Farms from the Death Tax and doubled the Child Tax Credit
- Obamacare individual mandate penalty GONE
- Under our tax cut, small businesses can now deduct 20 percent of their business income
- The Pledge to America's Workers has secured private-sector commitments to provide over 6.7 million jobs and training opportunities to American workers
- Reauthorized and modernized the Perkins Career and Technical Education Bill
- Announced a historic U.S.-Mexico-Canada Trade Agreement to replace NAFTA
- Concluded a tremendous new trade deal with South Korea and will begin trade negotiations with Japan to open new markets for American workers and farmers
- Reached a breakthrough agreement with the EU to increase U.S. exports
- Imposed tariffs on foreign steel & aluminum to protect our national security

- Imposed tariffs on China in response to China's intellectual property theft, forced technology transfer, and its chronically abusive trade practices
- Confirmed Supreme Court Justices Neil Gorsuch and Brett Kavanaugh
- Confirmed more circuit court judges than any other new administration
- Helped win U.S. bid for the 2028 Summer Olympics in Los Angeles
- Helped win U.S.-Mexico-Canada's united bid for 2026 World Cup
- Opened ANWR & approved Keystone XL and Dakota Access Pipelines
- Record number of regulations eliminated, saving $33 billion dollars
- Enacted regulatory relief for community banks and credit unions
- Made more affordable healthcare options available for Americans through association health plans and short-term limited duration plans
- Prescription drug prices declined in 2018, the first time in nearly half a century
- In 2017 and 2018, the FDA approved more affordable, generic drugs than ever before; many drug companies are freezing or reversing planned price increases
- Signed legislation to end "gag" clauses so patients can find the lowest priced drugs

- Passed Right to Try to give critically ill patients access to more life-saving cures
- Reformed the Medicare program to stop hospitals from overcharging seniors on their drugs—saving seniors hundreds of millions of dollars in 2018 alone
- Secured $6 billion in funding to fight the opioid epidemic
- Reduced high-dose opioid prescriptions by 16 percent during my first year in office
- Signed historic Veterans Affairs Choice legislation and the VA Accountability Act
- Expanded VA telehealth services, walk-in-clinics, same-day urgent primary and mental healthcare, and launched the promised 24-hour Veteran Hotline
- Signed an executive order to help prevent veteran suicide
- Increased coal exports by more than 60 percent during my first year in office
- The U.S. is the largest producer of oil and natural gas—surpassing Saudi Arabia and Russia. We are a net exporter of natural gas for the first time since 1957.
- Announced our withdrawal from the job-killing Paris Climate Accord
- Canceled the illegal, anti-coal, so-called Clean Power Plan
- Signed a bipartisan Criminal Justice Reform bill into law

- Secured a record $700 billion dollars in military funding; $716 billion this year
- Secured a $100 billion dollar increase in defense spending from NATO allies
- Launched whole-of-government approach to women's economic empowerment around the world (W-GDP) with a goal of empowering 50 million women by 2025
- Nuclear and ballistic missile testing in North Korea have stopped, hostages have been released, and the remains of our fallen warriors were returned home
- Began process to make the Space Force the 6th branch of the armed forces
- Initiated withdrawal from the Intermediate-Range Nuclear Forces (INF) Treaty
- Withdrew from the one-sided Iran Deal and imposed the toughest sanctions ever
- First country to recognize Juan Guaidó as interim president of Venezuela
- Recognized Jerusalem as the capital of Israel and moved the U.S. embassy
- Took historic action to recognize Israel's sovereignty over the Golan Heights
- Protecting Americans from terrorists with the travel ban, upheld by Supreme Court
- ISIS has been driven out from all territory they once held in Iraq and Syria
- Issued executive order to keep open Guantanamo Bay

- Improved vetting for refugees and switched focus to overseas settlement
- We have begun building the Wall and support strong borders and no crime

WE CAN WIN BECAUSE THE TRUTH IS ON OUR SIDE

The war for America's soul is a war between the forces of order and the forces of chaos and anarchy.

We can win. And we MUST win. We can win because of the indefatigable power of truth. Sooner or later lies are exposed, and liars stumble and are caught in the act of dissembling.

But how do you guarantee your access to the truth in the age of Fake News? How can you navigate media waters infested with propagandists and political activists masquerading as "journalists"?

Do what I do, and rely on sources of information that are tried and tested, people and platforms that have proven themselves patriotic defenders of the truth and American values.

I get most of my daily information from talk radio and podcasts, with Rush Limbaugh, Sean Hannity, Mark Levin, Dennis Prager, Mike Gallagher, Larry Elder, and my other Salem Radio colleagues at the top of the list.

But where else can you get the trustworthy analysis and fact-based reporting that you need to make the right arguments to support President Trump and our Make America Great Again agenda? In addition to tuning in to my national show *AMERICA First*, available at SebGorka.com and as a free podcast on the iTunes smartphone app, you can do what I do and turn to the best sources of information available on the Internet today.

These are outlets that cover a wide array of topics, from politics and culture to entertainment and history, all with a devotion to conservatism and our great nation. Below are the thirteen most important sources I use to inform myself and prepare every day for my show and public appearances. These are platforms you can rely upon to give you the unvarnished truth about the threats we face and how the president is succeeding against them. These sources are indispensable to members of Team MAGA. Use them.

1. **Breitbart News** (Breitbart.com, Twitter: @BreitbartNews): What Fox News is to television, Breitbart is to online media, or "alternative media." The website bearing the name of one of the greatest culture warriors in history has become a media war machine in its own right, years after Andrew Breitbart's tragic and early passing. It was on the front lines of the 2016 election, even working its way into Hillary Clinton's mind as an "alt-right" boogeyman, just proving how truly effective the site was and still is today. Breitbart boasts some of the sharpest and wittiest writers

on the Internet, including Matt Boyle (@mboyle1), John Nolte (@NolteNC), Joel B. Pollak (@joelpollak), and Allum Bokhari (@LibertarianBlue)

2. **American Greatness** (AmGreatness.com, Twitter: @theamgreatness): For a website that is only a few years old, American Greatness has already made an incredible impact in the world of right-wing commentary. This journal unapologetically attacks political correctness, directly takes on the Left in the battle for our culture, and also has plenty of time to rip into the Never-Trumpers of "Conservatism Inc." for their role in allowing the Left to become so dominant in the first place. American Greatness features such star-studded contributors as Dennis Prager (@DennisPrager), Candace Owens (@RealCandaceO), Victor Davis Hanson (@VDHanson), and Donald Trump Jr. (@DonaldJTrumpJr), as well as senior contributors such as Chris Buskirk (@thechrisbuskirk), Julie Kelly (@julie_kelly2), and me!

3. **Human Events** (HumanEvents.com, Twitter: @HumanEvents): The newly revamped version of the classic magazine, which was President Ronald Reagan's favorite publication, has exploded onto the scene in spectacular fashion. After being purchased and relaunched earlier this year, Human Events has taken on a more firmly nationalist, populist, and pro-Trump tone that is fitting for the era. With a combination of the same eloquence, research, and depth of topics as such publications as the *Claremont Review of Books*, and the same politically incorrect and bold tone of Breitbart and American Greatness, this new and improved site has everything

that is needed to take the fight directly to the Left in every way possible. Already skyrocketing in popularity, much to the ire of faux conservatives like Bill Kristol, Human Events has the strength, collection of talent, and resources to become the next big online publication that is truly just as much of a cultural weapon as it is a magazine, potentially as crucial to 2020 as Breitbart was to 2016. Its best and brightest minds include its editors Raheem Kassam (@RaheemKassam) and Will Chamberlain (@willchamberlain), as well as others like Ian Miles Cheong (@stillgray).

4. **The Daily Wire** (Dailywire.com, Twitter: @realDailyWire): Founded and run by Breitbart alum Ben Shapiro (@benshapiro), The Daily Wire features excellent commentary from such fighters as Michael Knowles (@michaeljknowles) and entertaining podcasts from Andrew Klavan, both of whom have been guests on *AMERICA First*. It also features contributors like Ryan Saavedra (@RealSaavedra), who is always on top of the media cycle with the latest breaking news around the clock. The Daily Wire continues to regularly demonstrate its motto: "Facts don't care about your feelings."

5. **The Federalist** (TheFederalist.com, Twitter: @FDRLST): If you ever want some good long-form articles on the topics of the day, the Federalist is a safe bet. It also holds the distinction of having perhaps the greatest collection of extensive, in-depth investigative articles on the scandal behind Operation Crossfire Hurricane, including the FISA abuses, corruption in the FBI,

and Deep State surveillance, among many, many other stories the legacy media doesn't want you to know about. Some of the best contributors include Sean Davis (@seanmdav), Mollie Hemingway (@MZHemingway), David Harsanyi (@davidharsanyi), and Ben Domenech (@bdomenech).

6. **Claremont Review of Books** (Claremont.org, Twitter: @ClaremontInst): The publication arm of the excellent Claremont Institute, the CRB features some of the most erudite language on the Internet and takes the deepest of dives into our history and the philosophical foundations of our Republic. Their articles put our current socio-political climate into a broader context and also offer suggestions as to where our country should be heading. If you ever want to feel as if you are in a library, reading the finest collection of highly intellectual content available, CRB will provide you with just that. Some of the best authors include Robert Reilly and the Heritage Foundation's David Azerrad.

7. **The Daily Signal** (DailySignal.com, Twitter: @DailySignal): "The Mothership of Conservatism," the Heritage Foundation has its very own fantastic publication in the Daily Signal, which covers a wide array of topics including our progress in the culture war. The outlet showcases the best minds that Heritage has to offer, as well as many of my radio guests on *AMERICA First*, including James Carafano (@JJCarafano), Jarrett Stepman (@JarrettStepman), Hans von Spakovsky (@HvonSpakovsky), and editor-in-chief Rob Bluey (@RobertBluey).

8. **The Daily Caller** (DailyCaller.com, Twitter: @DailyCaller): Perhaps no other site on the Internet does a better job of belting out dozens upon dozens of articles and videos every single day about the latest breaking news topics. From exclusive interviews and scoops to insightful commentary, the Daily Caller is a guaranteed source of the latest in our world, every hour of every day. Stephanie Hamill (@StephmHamill) is one of their star contributors.

9. **Townhall** (Townhall.com, Twitter: @townhallcom): Another member of the Salem Media family, Townhall features some of the best columns you will ever read, with an equal balance of going after the Left and tearing into fake "conservatives" who are anti-Trump or who otherwise harm the broader conservative agenda. Some of their best writers include "Colonel K." Kurt Schlichter (@KurtSchlichter), Fox News regular Katie Pavlich (@KatiePavlich), and the podcast team "Triggered" (@TriggeredTHM).

10. **The Washington Times** (WashingtonTimes.com, Twitter: @WashTimes): The *Washington Times* is perhaps the quintessential exemplar of what a balanced, unbiased media outlet should look like. This daily newspaper covers all the latest breaking news and showcases great commentary from such writers as Charlie Hurt (@CharlesHurt) and Stephen Moore (@StephenMoore). It has the budget and professional appearance of the nation's largest newspapers, but with none of the Fake News.

11. **PJ Media** (PJmedia.com, Twitter: @PJMedia_com): A member of our great Salem Media family, PJ Media is where you can find some of the most hard-hitting commentary against the Left, unapologetically going after some of the most radical Democrats in America today. In addition to politics, PJ Media covers issues of faith and culture, which are crucial to our ultimate success.

12. **City Journal** (City-Journal.org, Twitter: @CityJournal): *City Journal* features excellent long-form articles on just about everything, from culture to technology, from the economy to geo-politics, and from the founding principles of Western Civilization to the most relevant political issues of the day. The *Journal*'s vast stable of contributors even crosses the Atlantic to include great minds like Sir Roger Scruton (@Roger_Scruton).

13. **Newsbusters** (NewsBuster.org, Twitter: @NewsBusters): When there's liberal bias in the media, who are you gonna call? Newsbusters regularly publishes content featuring the most absurd statements and downright lies by Leftists in the Fake News Industrial Complex, including video clips and full transcripts. If you ever need to grab a ridiculous quote from MSNBC or CNN, this is surely the best place to go.

APPENDIX THREE

HILLARY CLINTON, SAUL ALINKSY, AND THE CONTINUING RELEVANCE OF *RULES FOR RADICALS*

S
aul Alinsky is the most important figure on the American Left in the last century, and the most formative political thinker for both Barack Obama and Hillary Clinton. It is telling that one of the few photographs available of "law professor" Obama has him diagramming Alinksy's theories on a chalkboard. Likewise, it is equally telling that the dissertation Hillary Clinton wrote at Wellesley was about Saul Alinksy and his tactics for taking power in a democracy.

In mapping the Democrat party's radical swing to the Left, and the rise to prominence of true socialist extremists like Alexandria Ocasio-Cortez, it is crucial that you understand the central role of

Saul Alinsky and his strategy for taking control of political systems through inside subversion.

To that end, I am including here key passages of Hillary's 1969 dissertation, "There is Only the Fight." (If you want to read more, Clinton's full thesis is available at: https://www.hillaryclintonquarterly.com/documents/HillaryClintonThesis.pdf).[1]

As you read Hillary's words, just remember this, Alinksy dedicated his book *Rules for Radicals* to the first revolutionary, the Devil:

> Lest we forget at least an over-the-shoulder acknowledgment to the very first radical: from all our legends, mythology, and history (and who is to know where mythology leaves off and history begins— or which is which), the first radical known to man who rebelled against the establishment and did it so effectively that he at least won his own kingdom

> —Lucifer.

—SAUL ALINSKY

"THERE IS ONLY THE FIGHT..."

An Analysis of the Alinsky Model

A thesis submitted in partial fulfillment
of the requirements for the Bachelor of Arts
degree under the Special Honors Program,
Wellesley College, Wellesley, Massachusetts.

Hillary D. Rodham
Political Science
2 May, 1969

194

TABLE OF CONTENTS

ACKNOWLEDGEMENTS

Although I have no "loving wife" to thank for keeping
the children away while I wrote, I do have many friends and
teachers who have contributed to the process of thesis-writing.
And I thank them for their tireless help and encouragement. In
regard to the paper itself, there are three people who deserve
special appreciation: Mr. Alinsky for providing a topic, sharing
his time and offering me a job; Miss Alona E. Evans for her
thoughtful questioning and careful editing that clarified fuzzy
thinking and tortured prose; and Jan Krigbaum for her spirited
intellectual companionship and typewriter rescue work.

hdr

CHAPTER I

SAUL DAVID ALINSKY: AN AMERICAN RADICAL

With customary British understatement, The Economist referred
to Saul Alinsky as "that rare specimen, the successful radical."[1] This
is one of the blander descriptions applied to Alinsky during a thirty-
year career in which epithets have been collected more regularly than
paychecks. The epithets are not surprising as most people who deal with
Alinsky need to categorize in order to handle him. It is far easier to
cope with a man if, depending on ideological perspective, he is classified as a "crackpot" than to grapple with the substantive issues he pre-
sents. For Saul Alinsky is more than a man who has created a particular
approach to community organizing, he is the articulate proponent of wha[t]
many consider to be a dangerous socio/political philosophy. An understanding of the "Alinsky-type method" (i.e. his organizing method) as
well as the philosophy on which it is based must start with an understanding of the man himself.

Alinsky was born in a Chicago slum to Russian Jewish immigrant
parents, and these early conditions of slum living and poverty in Chicago established the context of his ideas and mode of action. He traces
his identification with the poor back to a home in the rear of a store
where his idea of luxury was using the bathroom without a customer bang-
ing on the door.[2] Chicago itself has also greatly influenced him:

> Where did I come from? Chicago. I can curse and hate the town
> but let anyone else do it and they're in for a battle. There I've
> had the happiest and the worst times of my life. Every street has
> its personal joy and pain to me. On this street is the church of
> a Catholic Bishop who was a big part of my life; further down is
> another church where the pastor too has meant a lot to me; and a
> couple miles away is a cemetery—well, skip it. Many Chicago street

His answer is prefaced by pages of Fourth-of-July rhetoric about
Americans: "They are a people creating a new bridge of mankind in between
the past of narrow nationalistic chauvinism and the horizon of a new man-
kind--a people of the world." Although the book was written right after
World War II, which deeply affected Alinsky, his belief in American democracy has deep historical roots--at least, as he interprets history:

> The American people were, in the beginning, Revolutionaries and
> Tories. The American People ever since have been Revolutionaries
> and Tories...regardless of the labels of the past and present...
> The clash of Radicals, Conservatives, and Liberals which makes
> up America's political history opens the door to the most funda-
> mental question of What is America? How do the people of America
> feel? There were and are a number of Americans--few, to be sure--
> filled with deep feelings for people. They know that people are the
> stuff that makes up the dream of democracy. These few were and are
> the American Radicals and the only way we can understand the Amer-
> ican Radical is to understand what we mean by this feeling for and
> with the people.7

What Alinsky means by this "feeling for and with the people" is
simply how much one person really cares about people unlike himself. He
illustrates the feeling by a series of examples in which he poses questions
such as: So you are a white, native-born Protestant. Do you like people?
He then proceeds to demonstrate how, in spite of protestations, the Protestant (or the Irish Catholic or the Jew or the Negro or the Mexican) only
pays lip service to the idea of equality. This technique of confrontation
in Alinsky's writing effectively involves most of his readers who will
recognize in themselves at least one of the characteristics he denounces.
Having confronted his readers with their hypocrisy, Alinsky defines the
American Radical as "...that unique person who actually believes what he
says...to whom the common good is the greatest personal value...who gen-
uinely and completely believes in mankind...."

> What does the Radical want? He wants a world in which the worth
> of the individual is recognized...a world based on the morality of
> mankind...The Radical believes that all peoples should have a high
> standard of food, housing,and health...The Radical places human
> rights far above property rights. He is for universal,free public
> education and recognizes this as fundamental to the democratic way
> of life...Democracy to him is working from the bottom up...The Radical
> believes completely in real equality of opportunity for all peoples
> regardless of race, color, or creed.11

Much of what Alinsky professes does not sound "radical." His are the words
used in our schools and churches, by our parents and their friends, by our
peers. The difference is that Alinsky really believes in them and recognizes the necessity of changing the present structures of our lives in
order to realize them.

There are many inconsistencies in Alinsky's thought which he himself
recognizes and dismisses. He believes that life is inconsistent and that
one needs flexibility in dealing with its many facets. His writings reflect
the flavor of inconsistency which permeates his approach to organizing. They
also suggest Alinsky's place in the American Radical tradition. In order
to discuss his place, it is necessary to circumvent his definition of "radical" based on inner psychological strength and commitment, and to consider
more conventional uses of the term.

Although there is great disagreement among writers about the definition of "radical" and among radicals themselves over the scope of the
word's meaning, there is sufficient agreement to permit a general definition.
A radical is one who advocates sweeping changes in the existing laws and
methods of government. These proposed changes are aimed at the roots of
political problems which in Marxian terms are the attitudes and the behaviors
of men. Radicals are not interested in ameliorating the symptoms of decay
but in drastically altering the causes of societal conditions. Radicalism
"emphasizes reason rather than reverence, although Radicals have often been
the most emotional and least reasonable of men."12

corrupt evil, unhealthy immoral Machiavellianism, and a general
phantasmagoria of the nether regions.16

For Alinsky, power is the "very essence of life, the dynamic of life" and
is found in "...active citizen participation pulsing upward providing a
unified strength for a common purpose of organization...either changing
circumstances or opposing change."[17]

Alinsky argues that those who wish to change circumstances must
develop a mass-based organization and be prepared for conflict. He is a
neo-Hobbesian who objects to the consensual mystique surrounding political
processes; for him, conflict is the route to power. Those possessing power
want to retain it and often to extend the bounds of it. Those desiring a
change in the power balance generally lack the established criteria of money
or status and so must mobilize numbers. Mobilized groups representing opposed interests will naturally be in conflict which Alinsky considers a
healthful and necessary aspect of a community organizing activity. He is
supported in his prognosis by conflict analysts such as Lewis Coser who
points out in The Functions of Social Conflict that:

> Conflict with other groups contributes to the establishment and
> reaffirmation of the group and maintains its boundaries against the
> surrounding social world.18

In order to achieve a world without bounds it appears essential for many
groups to solidify their identities both in relation to their own membership
and to their external environment. This has been the rationale of nationalist groups historically and among American blacks presently.

The organizer plays a significant role in precipitating and directing
a community's conflict pattern. As Alinsky views this role, the organizer
is

> ...dedicated to changing the character of life of a particular community
> [and] has an initial function of serving as an abrasive agent to rub
> raw the resentments of the people of the community; to fan latent hos-

200

CHAPTER II

THE ALINSKY METHOD OF ORGANIZING: THREE CASE STUDIES

The Alinsky method of community organizing has two distinct
elements. One, the "Alinsky-type protest" is "an explosive mixture of
rigid discipline, brilliant showmanship, and a street fighter's instinct
for ruthlessly exploiting his enemy's weakness."[1] The second, modelled
after trade union organization methods, involves the hard work of rec-
ognizing interests, seeking out indigenous leaders, and building an
organization whose power is viewed as legitimate by the larger community. It is difficult to discuss these two components separately because they are woven into the organizational pattern according to sit-
uational necessity. Some organizational situations need the polarizing
effect of "rubbing raw the sores of discontent" while others with well-
defined resentments need leaders.

Another distinctive feature of the Alinsky method as mentioned
in the previous chapter is the use of military language. As Silberman
points out, such language is appropriate for groups engaged in "war-like"
struggles for

> ...the only way to build an army is by winning a few victories.
> But how do you gain a victory before you have an army? The only
> method ever devised is guerrilla warfare: to avoid a fixed battle
> where the forces are arrayed and where the new army's weakness
> would become visible, and to concentrate instead on hit-and-run
> tactics designed to gain small but measurable victories. Hence the
> emphasis on such dramatic actions as parades and rent strikes whose
> main objective is to create a sense of solidarity and community.[2]

Although Alinsky's goal of community solidarity and his war on power-
lessness has been co-opted into the rubric of the federal welfare pro-
grams, there is a continuing mistrust of his tactics. As has been sug-

Discussing Alinsky's tactics apart from his actions is like discussing current theories of international relations without mentioning Vietnam. We will consider three of the organizations which Alinsky helped build.

The first of the three is the Back of the Yards Neighborhood Council which is the prototype community organization dating back to the late 1930's. Alinsky's involvement with the Council led to the establishment of the Industrial Areas Foundation which subsequently coordinated other organizing activities. One of the most important of these was The Woodlawn Organization, a black community group in Chicago. Alinsky frequently encounters blacks who view Alinsky's efforts as just one more example of white man's power politics game. He tells such critics that,"Sunglasses, Swahili, and soul food won't win power for blacks."[4] Thirdly,we will look at the organizational problems involved in the Rochester black community's confrontation with the Kodak Company.

THE BACK OF THE YARDS NEIGHBORHOOD COUNCIL

Upton Sinclair's novel, The Jungle, focused attention on the stockyards in Chicago and the deplorable conditions of life in the area surrounding the Yards. This area, Back of the Yards, was bigamously wedded to the meat-packing industry and the Roman Catholic Church. The meat factories provided jobs and the Church ministered to the spiritual and social needs of its parishoners. The waves of Polish, Slovak, and Irish immigrants before World War I and Mexican immigration after, supplied both workers and parishoners. The immigrants also successively lowered the wage scale and fragmented the Church into bickering nationalistic divisions. The area's depressed economy was accompanied by acute environmental problems such as overcrowded housing, insufficient sanitation, unpaved streets, few recreational facilities, high delinquency and crime rates, and inadequate schools.[5] Alinsky remembers the Back of the Yards as "the nadir of American Slums, worse than Harlem."[6]

NOTES

PREFACE: What the Left Has Wrought

1. "The Mission of the Churchill Institute," Churchill Institute, https://thecinst.org/our-mission/.

2. Douglas Ernst, "Trinity College Defends Professor's 'Whiteness Is Terrorism' Message," *Washington Times*, April 29, 2019, https://www.washingtontimes.com/news/2019/apr/29/johnny-eric-williams-trinity-college-professor-whi/.

3. Tyler O'Neil, "Professor Calls Whites 'Inhuman A**holes,' Tells Blacks to 'Let Them F*cking Die,'" PJ Media, June 21, 2017, https://pjmedia.com/trending/2017/06/21/prof-calls-whites-inhuman-aholes-tells-blacks-to-let-them-fcking-die/.

CHAPTER ONE: OBAMAGATE: THE ATTEMPTED COUP AGAINST DONALD J. TRUMP

1. Tim Hains, "Flashback June 2015: Bill Maher and His Audience Laugh at Ann Coulter for Saying Trump Could Win Nomination," RealClearPolitics, May 4, 2016, https://www.realclearpolitics.com/video/2016/05/04/flashback_june_2015_bill_maher__his_audience_laugh_at_ann_coulter_for_saying_trump_could_win.html.

2. Adam Shaw, "Sessions Defends Decision To Recuse Himself from Russian Probe," FOX News, March 10, 2018, https://www.foxnews.com/politics/sessions-defends-decision-to-recuse-himself-from-russian-probe.

3. William Barr, "William Barr Interview: Read the Full Transcript," interview by Jan Crawford, *CBS This Morning*, CBS, May 31, 2019, transcript, https://www.cbsnews.com/news/william-barr-interview-full-transcript-cbs-this-morning-jan-crawford-exclusive-2019-05-31/.

4. Jeff Mordock, "William Barr Appoints U.S. Attorney To Investigate Russia Probe Origins," *Washington Examiner*, May 13, 2019, https://www.washingtontimes.com/news/2019/may/13/john-durham-appointed-william-barr-investigate-rus/.

5. "John H. Durham Sworn in as United States Attorney," News and Press Releases, United States Department of Justice, February 22, 2018, https://www.justice.gov/usao-ct/pr/john-h-durham-sworn-united-states-attorney.

6. T.J. Singh, "Dan Bongino—Obama, Mueller, and the Biggest Scam in U.S. History," filmed November 22, 2018, at the David Horowitz Freedom Center Restoration Weekend, https://www.youtube.com/watch?v=_aevtHHULag.

7. Guy Benson, "Fact Check: No, New IG Report Doesn't Prove IRS Targeting Scandal Was a Right-Wing 'Myth,'" *Townhall*, October 30, 2017, https://townhall.com/tipsheet/guybenson/2017/10/30/no-liberals-the-irs-targeting-scandal-is-not-a-rightwing-myth-n2402022.

8. Christopher Goffard, "Archives Show Nixon's Targeting of Foes," *Los Angeles Times*, December 3, 2008, https://www.latimes.com/archives/la-xpm-2008-dec-03-na-nixon3-story.html.

9. "Vindictive Shutdown Theater," *National Review*, October 7, 2013, ttps://www.nationalreview.com/2013/10/vindictive-shutdown-theater-editors/.

10. Philip Bump, "Fox News Reporter May Face Criminal Charges for Reporting on the CIA," *The Atlantic*, May 20, 2013, https://www.theatlantic.com/politics/archive/2013/05/fox-news-reporter-james-rosen-may-face-criminal-charges-reporting-cia/315087/.

11. C. Mitchell Shaw, "Sharyl Attkisson: IG's Office Swapped Out my Hard Drive after Fed Agents Hacked my Computer," *The New American*, March 8, 2018, https://www.thenewamerican.com/usnews/crime/item/28455-sharyl-attkisson-igs-office-swapped-out-my-hard-drive-after-fed-agents-hacked-my-computer.

12. Jon Greenberg, "CNN's Tapper: Obama Has Used Espionage Act More Than All Previous Administrations," PunditFact, PolitiFact, January 10, 2014, https://www.politifact.com/punditfact/statements/2014/jan/10/jake-tapper/cnns-tapper-obama-has-used-espionage-act-more-all-/.

13. "What We Do Know about the Benghazi Attack Demands a Reckoning," *National Review*, June 28, 2016, https://www.nationalreview.com/2016/06/benghazi-scandal-hillary-clinton-state-department-obama-administration-house-committee/.

14.   Tom Bevan, "What the President Said about Benghazi,"
      RealClearPolitics, November 30, 2012, https://www.realclearpolitics.
      com/articles/2012/11/30/what_the_president_said_about_
      benghazi_116299.html.

15.   Juan Williams, "Where's the Outrage Over Obama's Drone Policy?"
      Fox News, February 7, 2013, https://www.foxnews.com/opinion/
      wheres-the-outrage-over-obamas-drone-policy.

16.   Juan Williams, "Where's the Outrage over Obama's Drone Policy?"
      Fox News, February 7, 2013, https://www.foxnews.com/opinion/
      wheres-the-outrage-over-obamas-drone-policy.

17.   Richi Jennings, "NSA's Huge Utah Datacenter: How Much of Your
      Data Will It Store? Experts Disagree...." *Forbes*, July 26, 2013, https://
      www.forbes.com/sites/netapp/2013/07/26/nsa-utah-
      datacenter/#3af05c085d9c.

18.   Bruce Upbin, "The Web Is Much Bigger (and Smaller) Than You
      Think," *Forbes*, April 24, 2012, https://www.forbes.com/sites/
      ciocentral/2012/04/24/the-web-is-much-bigger-and-smaller-than-you-
      think/#32c6696d7619.

19.   Philip Bump, "The NSA Admits It Analyzes More People's Data Than
      Previously Revealed," *The Atlantic*, July 17, 2013, https://www.
      theatlantic.com/politics/archive/2013/07/nsa-admits-it-analyzes-more-
      peoples-data-previously-revealed/313220/.

20.   Amy Nordrum, "NSA Can Legally Access Metadata of 25,000 Callers
      Based on a Single Suspect's Phone," Security, IEEE Spectrum, May 16,
      2016, https://spectrum.ieee.org/tech-talk/telecom/security/nsa-can-
      legally-access-metadata-of-25000-callers-based-on-a-single-suspects-
      phone-analysis-suggests.

21. Siobhan Gorman, "NSA Collects 20% or Less of U.S. Call Data," *Wall Street Journal*, February 7, 2014, https://www.wsj.com/articles/nsa-collects-20-or-less-of-us-call-data-1391790665.

22. "Protecting U.S. Person Identities in Disseminations under the Foreign Intelligence Surveillance Act," Office of Civil Liberties, Privacy, and Transparency; Office of the Director of National Intelligence, November 2017, https://www.dni.gov/files/documents/icotr/CLPT-USP-Dissemination-Paper—-FINAL-clean-11.17.17.pdf.

23. Tim Hains, "Dan Bongino on Spygate: Obama, Mueller, and the Biggest Spy Scandal in American History," RealClearPolitics, November 25, 2018, https://www.realclearpolitics.com/video/2018/11/25/dan_bongino_on_spygate_obama_mueller__the_biggest_spy_scandal_in_american_history.html.

24. Deb Reichmann, "Report: Government Officials 'Unmasked' More Than 1,900 Americans Swept Up in Foreign Surveillance," *PBS News Hour*, May 2, 2017, https://www.pbs.org/newshour/nation/report-government-officials-unmasked-1900-americans-swept-foreign-surveillance.

25. Sara Carter, "ODNI and NSA Impede Lawmakers Review of Obama Admin 'Unmasking' Requests," *SaraACarter.com*, February 19, 2019, https://saraacarter.com/odni-and-nsa-impede-lawmakers-review-of-obama-admin-unmasking-requests/.

26. "Who Is Adm. Mike Rogers? Unsung 'Hero' Alerted President Trump to Illegal Spying," *World Tribune*, May 1, 2019, https://www.worldtribune.com/who-is-adm-mike-rogers-unsung-hero-alerted-president-trump-to-illegal-spying/.

27. "50 U.S. Code §1801. Definitions," U.S. Code, Legal Information Institute, July 11, 2019, https://www.law.cornell.edu/uscode/text/50/1801.

28. John Solomon, "FISA Shocker: DOJ Official Warned Steele Dossier Was Connected to Clinton, Might Be Biased," *The Hill*, January 16, 2019, https://thehill.com/opinion/white-house/425739-fisa-shocker-doj-official-warned-steele-dossier-was-connected-to-clinton.

29. Andrew C. McCarthy, "Explosive Revelation of Obama Administration Illegal Surveillance of Americas," *National Review*, May 25, 2017, https://www.nationalreview.com/2017/05/nsa-illegal-surveillance-americans-obama-administration-abuse-fisa-court-response/.

30. Jeff Carlson, "NSA Director Rogers Disclosed FISA Abuse Days after Page Warrant Was Issued," *Epoch Times*, June 18, 2019, https://www.theepochtimes.com/nsa-director-rogers-disclosed-fisa-abuse-days-after-carter-page-fisa-was-issued_2692033.html.

31. S. A. Miller, "Donald Trump Moves Transition Meetings to Private Golf Club in New Jersey," *Washington Times*, November 1, 2016, https://www.washingtontimes.com/news/2016/nov/17/donald-trump-moves-transition-meetings-private-gol/.

32. Donald J. Trump (@realDonaldTrump), "Terrible! Just Found Out That Obama Had My 'Wires Tapped' in Trump Tower," Twitter, March 4, 2017, https://twitter.com/realdonaldtrump/status/837989835818287106?lang=en.

33. Allen Cone, "Obama Officials Want NSA Chief, Possible Trump Cabinet Pick Mike Rogers Fired," UPI, November 21, 2016, https://www.upi.com/Top_News/US/2016/11/20/Obama-officials-want-NSA-chief-possible-Trump-Cabinet-pick-Mike-Rogers-fired/7441479653208/.

34. Kimberley Strassel, "Brennan and the 2016 Spy Scandal," *Wall Street Journal*, July 19, 2018, https://www.wsj.com/articles/brennan-and-the-2016-spy-scandal-1532039346.

35. George Neumayr, "The London-to-Langley Spy Ring," *American Spectator*, May 25, 2018, https://spectator.org/the-london-to-langley-spy-ring/.

36. Shane Harris, "John Brennan, the Triumphant Bureaucrat," *Washingtonian*, February 8, 2013, https://www.washingtonian.com/2013/02/08/john-brennan-the-triumphant-bureaucrat/.

37. Andrew C. McCarthy, "The Steele Dossier and the 'Verified Application' That Wasn't," *National Review*, May 18, 2019, https://www.nationalreview.com/2019/05/the-steele-dossier-and-the-verified-application-that-wasn't.

38. John Solomon, "Steele's Stunning Pre-FISA Confession: Informant Needed to Air Trump Dirt before Election," *The Hill*, May 7, 2019, https://thehill.com/opinion/white-house/442592-steeles-stunning-pre-fisa-confession-informant-needed-to-air-trump-dirt.

39. Jonathan Turley, "The Steele Dossier and the Perils of Political Insurance Policies," *The Hill*, December 22, 2018, https://thehill.com/opinion/criminal-justice/422592-steeles-curious-comments-suggest-dossier-was-insurance-plan.

40. Jenny Beth Martin, "Trump's Accusers Harmed Us All. Hold Them Accountable," RealClearPolitics, March 29, 2019, https://www.realclearpolitics.com/articles/2019/03/29/trumps_accusers_harmed_us_all_hold_them_accountable_139889.html.

41. Tim Hains, "Dan Bongino on Spygate: Obama, Mueller, and the Biggest Spy Scandal in American History," RealClearPolitics, November 25, 2018, https://www.realclearpolitics.com/video/2018/11/25/dan_bongino_on_spygate_obama_mueller__the_biggest_spy_scandal_in_american_history.html.

42. Jeff Carlson, "Carter Page's Assistance in Russian Spy Case Might Count as Exculpatory Evidence," *Epoch Times*, September 10, 2018, https://www.theepochtimes.com/carter-pages-assistance-in-russian-spy-case-could-count-as-exculpatory-evidence_2656861.html.

43. Charlie Spiering, "Jeff Sessions Resigns as Attorney General," Breitbart, November 7, 2018, https://www.breitbart.com/politics/2018/11/07/jeff-sessions-resigns-as-donald-trump-attorney-general/.

44. "Appointment of Special Counsel to Investigate Russian Interferences with the 2016 Presidential Election and Related Matters," Office of the Deputy Attorney General, May 17, 2017, https://www.justice.gov/opa/press-release/file/967231/download.

45. Ronn Blitzer, "Mueller, Trump Clash over Whether He Sought FBI Job," Fox News, July 24, 2019, https://www.foxnews.com/politics/mueller-trump-clash-over-whether-he-sought-fbi-job.

46. Ronn Blitzer, "Legal Experts Stunned by DA's 'Barbaric' Move To Send Manafort to Rikers Island," Fox News, June 5, 2019, https://www.foxnews.com/politics/legal-experts-stunned-by-das-barbaric-decision-to-send-manafort-to-rikers-island.

47. Andrew C. McCarthy, "Flynn: Fact, and Narrative," *National Review*, December 19, 2018, https://www.nationalreview.com/2018/12/flynn-fact-and-narrative/.

48. "Mueller Finds No Collusion with Russia, Leaves Obstruction Question Open," American Bar Association, March 2019, https://www.americanbar.org/news/abanews/aba-news-archives/2019/03/mueller-concludes-investigation/.

49. James Comey, "Statement by FBI Director James B. Comey on the Investigation of Secretary Hillary Clinton's Use of a Personal E-Mail System," Press Releases, FBI National Press Office, July 5, 2016, https://www.fbi.gov/news/pressrel/press-releases/statement-by-fbi-director-james-b-comey-on-the-investigation-of-secretary-hillary-clinton2019s-use-of-a-personal-e-mail-system.

50. "Special Counsel Robert S. Mueller III Makes Statement on Investigation into Russian Interference in the 2016 Presidential Election," Office of Public Affairs, News, the United States Department of Justice, May 29, 2019, https://www.justice.gov/opa/speech/special-counsel-robert-s-mueller-iii-makes-statement-investigation-russian-interference.

51. Alex Pappas, Judson Berger, "Tight-lipped Mueller Faces GOP Ire over Probe's Handling, As Hearing Retreads Russia Report," Fox News, July 24, 2019, https://www.foxnews.com/politics/mueller-in-capitol-hill-testimony-says-no-trump-russia-conspiracy-no-trump-exoneration-on-obstruction.

52. Sean Davis, "Mueller Just Proved His Entire Operation Was A Political Hit Job That Trampled The Rule Of Law," Federalist, May 29, 2019, https://thefederalist.com/2019/05/29/mueller-just-proved-his-entire-operation-was-a-political-hit-job-that-trampled-the-rule-of-law/.

53. "Rule 3.8: Special Responsibilities of a Prosecutor," Model Rules of Professional Conduct, American Bar Association, July 11, 2019, https://www.americanbar.org/groups/professional_responsibility/publications/model_rules_of_professional_conduct/rule_3_8_special_responsibilities_of_a_prosecutor/.

54. Jessica Damiana, "Yes He Can: 'Clever Boy' Obama Returns to Indonesia for Family Vacation," Reuters, June 28, 2017, https://www.reuters.com/article/us-indonesia-usa-obama-idUSKBN19J1JT.

55. Paul Kengor, "Obama's Communist Mentor," *National Review*, October 5, 2010, https://www.nationalreview.com/2010/10/obamas-communist-mentor-paul-kengor.

56. Matt Patterson, "Study Saul Alinsky to Understand Barack Obama," *Washington Examiner*, February 6, 2012, https://www.washingtonexaminer.com/study-saul-alinsky-to-understand-barack-obama.

57. John Fund, "Obama's 'Chicago Way,'" *National Review*, May 30, 2013, https://www.nationalreview.com/2013/05/obamas-chicago-way-john-fund/.

58. Eric Levitz, "CIA Director Reveals He Was Once a Communist Sympathizer," *New York Magazine, Intelligencer*, September 22, 2016, http://nymag.com/intelligencer/2016/09/cia-director-reveals-he-was-once-a-communist-sympathizer.html.

59. Paul Kengor, "Comey Was a Commie," *American Spectator*, May 21, 2019, https://spectator.org/comey-was-a-commie/.

60. Josh Gerstein, "Hillary Clinton's Radical Summer," *New York Sun*, November 26, 2007, https://www.nysun.com/national/hillary-clintons-radical-summer/66933/.

61. Hillary D. Rodham, "'There Is Only the Fight…': An Analysis of the Alinsky Model," (B.A. thesis, Wellesley College, 1969), https://www.docdroid.net/V8962fC/hillaryclintonthesis.pdf.

62.

CHAPTER TWO: THE POLITICAL ELITE'S BIPARTISAN BETRAYAL OF AMERICA

1.   J. D. Vance, *Hillbilly Elegy: A Memoir of a Family and a Culture in Crisis* (New York: HarperCollins, 2016).

2.   Ibid, 22.

3.   Ibid, 18.

4.   William Egginton, *The Splintering of the American Mind: Identity Politics, Inequality, and Community on Today's College Campuses*, (London: Bloomsbury Publishing, 2018), 152.

5.   Vance, *Hillbilly Elegy*, 52.

6.   Ibid, 54.

7.   Ibid, 55.

8.   Michael van der Galien, "Bannon: 'Monday Was the Most Important Day of Trump's Presidency,'" PJ Media, May 7, 2019, https://pjmedia.com/trending/bannon-monday-was-the-most-important-day-of-trumps-presidency/.

9.   Steve Bannon, "An Hour with Steve Bannon, Former Chief Strategist to President Donald Trump," interview by Charlie Rose, Charlierose.com, September 11, 2017, https://charlierose.com/episodes/30951.

10. "Munk Debate on the Rise of Populism," C-SPAN, November 2, 2018, https://www.c-span.org/video/?453964-1/steve-bannon-david-frum-debate-rise-populism.

11. Damian Paletta and Caroline Porter, "Use of Food Stamps Swells Even as Economy Improves," *Wall Street Journal*, March 27, 2013, https://www.wsj.com/articles/SB10001424127887323699704578328601204933288.

12. Vance, *Hillbilly Elegy*, 144.

CHAPTER THREE: THE PLOTTERS—AND THEIR PLAN— TO DESTROY AMERICA

1. Dick Cheney and Liz Cheney, *Exceptional: Why the World Needs a Powerful America* (New York: Threshold Editions, 2015), 51.

2. Otis C. Mitchell, *The Cold War in Germany: Overview, Origins and Intelligence Wars* (Lanham, Maryland: University Press of America, 2005), 59.

3. Romesh Ratnesar, *Tear Down This Wall: A City, a President, and the Speech that Ended the Cold War,* (New York: Simon and Schuster, 2009), 4.

4. "Fatalities at the Berlin Wall: 1961–89," Berlin Wall Memorial, https://www.berliner-mauer-gedenkstaette.de/en/todesopfer-240.html.

5. Wesley Pruden, "The Four Noisy Horseladies of the Apocalypse," *Washington Times,* July 15, 2019, https://www.washingtontimes.com/news/2019/jul/15/alexandria-ocasio-cortez-her-squad-have-taken-over/.

6. Andrew Breitbart, *Righteous Indignation: Excuse Me While I Save the World!* (New York: Grand Central Publishing, 2011), 121.

7. Breitbart, *Righteous Indignation,* 125.

CHAPTER FOUR: CAN PRESIDENT TRUMP STOP THE RADICAL LEFT?

1. Byron York, "Harvard Study: CNN, NBC Trump Coverage 93 Percent Negative," *Washington Examiner,* May 19, 2017, https://www.washingtonexaminer.com/byron-york-harvard-study-cnn-nbc-trump-coverage-93-percent-negative.

2. Brooke Singman, "Special Counsel Mueller's Team Has Only One Known Republican," Fox News, February 23, 2018, https://www.foxnews.com/politics/special-counsel-muellers-team-has-only-one-known-republican.

3. John Gage, "Pelosi: 'We Cannot Accept a Second Term for Donald Trump,'" *Washington Examiner*, May 7, 2019, https://www. washingtonexaminer.com/news/pelosi-we-cannot-accept-a-second-term-for-donald-trump.
4. My conversations with Victor Davis Hanson, Lord Black, and, later in the book, President Trump, have been edited slightly for readability.
5. "Grassley, Graham Uncover 'Unusual Email' Sent by Susan Rice to Herself on President Trump's Inauguration Day," News Releases, Chuck Grassley U.S. Senator for Iowa website, February 12, 2018, https://www.grassley.senate.gov/news/news-releases/grassley-graham-uncover-unusual-email-sent-susan-rice-herself-president-trump-s.

CHAPTER FIVE: HOW YOU CAN WIN THE WAR FOR AMERICA'S SOUL

1. Paul Bedard, "Trump Campaign Mocks Bernie Sanders' Honeymoon to Soviet Union, 'What a Joke!'" *Washington Examiner*, May 28, 2019, https://www.washingtonexaminer.com/washington-secrets/trump-campaign-mocks-bernie-sanders-honeymoon-to-russia-what-a-joke.
2. Sun Tzu, *The Art of War*, translated by Lionel Giles, 2009, http://classics.mit.edu/Tzu/artwar.html.
3. "Reagan, a Wise Man Who Fooled Many People All of the Time," *The Telegraph*, February 6, 2001, https://www.telegraph.co.uk/comment/4259277/Reagan-a-wise-man-who-fooled-many-people-all-of-the-time.html.
4. Roger Simon, "Reclaiming the Culture," PJ Media, December 6, 2012, https://pjmedia.com/rogerlsimon/2012/12/06/reclaiming-the-culture/.

5.   Chen Guangcheng, *The Barefoot Lawyer: A Blind Man's Fight for Justice and Freedom in China*, (Henry Holt and Company, 2014).

BONUS CHAPTER SIX: STRAIGHT ANSWERS TO POPULAR QUESTIONS

1.   Andrew Walker and Josh Wester, "From Obamacare to *Obergefell*: The Obama Administration's Troubled Legacy on Religious Liberty," *National Review*, January 18, 2017, https://www.nationalreview.com/2017/01/obama-administration-has-troubled-religious-liberty-legacy/.

2.   Kira Goldenberg, "Obama's Broken Promises on Transparency," Columbia Journalism Review, October 10, 2013, https://archives.cjr.org/behind_the_news/cjp_report_on_us_press_freedom.php.

3.   Alina Polyakova and Filippos Letsas, "On the Record: The U.S. Administration's Actions on Russia," Brookings Institution, June 3, 2019, https://www.brookings.edu/blog/order-from-chaos/2018/09/25/on-the-record-the-u-s-administrations-actions-on-russia/.

4.   "President Trump's Speech to the Arab Islamic American Summit," Statements and Releases, the White House, May 21, 2017, https://www.whitehouse.gov/briefings-statements/president-trumps-speech-arab-islamic-american-summit/.

5.   John Gage, "Megan Rapinoe Says She Will Talk to Anyone Who 'Believes the Same Things We Believe In,'" *Washington Examiner,* July 10, 2019, https://www.washingtonexaminer.com/news/megan-rapinoe-says-she-will-talk-to-anyone-who-believes-the-same-things-we-believe-in.

6. Mosheh Oinounou and Bonney Kapp, "Michelle Obama Takes Heat for Saying She's 'Proud of My Country for the First Time,'" Fox News, February 19, 2008, https://www.foxnews.com/story/michelle-obama-takes-heat-for-saying-shes-proud-of-my-country-for-the-first-time.

7. "The Perils of Illegal Border Crossing," Press Releases, Department of Homeland Security, July 19, 2019, https://www.dhs.gov/news/2018/07/19/perils-illegal-border-crossing.

8. "Unaccompanied Alien Children and Family Units Are Flooding the Border Because of Catch and Release Loopholes," *Department of Homeland Security,* February 15, 2018, https://www.dhs.gov/news/2018/02/15/unaccompanied-alien-children-and-family-units-are-flooding-border-because-catch-and.

9. Avik Roy, "Man Bites Dog: Trump Did Better with Minorities in 2016 Than Mitt Romney Did in 2012," *Forbes,* November 19, 2016, https://www.forbes.com/sites/aviksaroy/2016/11/19/man-bites-dog-trump-did-better-with-minorities-than-mitt-romney-did-in-2012/.

10. Bill Powell, "How Rick Santorum Helped Donald Trump Win the White House," *Newsweek,* November 15, 2016, https://www.newsweek.com/2016/11/25/donald-trump-presidential-campaign-521145.html.

11. David Skolnick, "Trump's Victory in Mahoning Valley Is One for Record Books," *The Vindicator,* November 9, 2016, https://www.vindy.com/news/2016/nov/09/trump-fares-well-across-valley/.

BONUS CHAPTER SEVEN: AN EXCLUSIVE INTERVIEW WITH PRESIDENT DONALD TRUMP

1. Paul Bedard, "Heritage Foundation: 64% of Trump's Agenda Already Done, Faster Than Reagan," *Washington Examiner,* February 27, 2018, https://www.washingtonexaminer.com/heritage-foundation-64-of-trumps-agenda-already-done-faster-than-reagan.

2. See the following document: TRUMP ADMINISTRATION ACCOMPLISHMENTS.

3. Freddy Gray, "In 2016, Paul Krugman Said the Markets Would 'Never Recover' from Trump's Victory. Ha!" *The Spectator*, August 28, 2018, https://spectator.us/2016-paul-krugman-markets-never-recover-trumps-victory-ha/.

APPENDIX THREE: HILLARY CLINTON, SAUL ALINKSY, AND THE CONTINUING RELEVANCE OF RULES FOR RADICALS

1. Hillary Clinton, "There Is Only the Fight: An Analysis of the Alinsky Model," (Bachelor of Arts thesis, Wellesley College, 1969), https://www.hillaryclintonquarterly.com/documents/HillaryClintonThesis.pdf.

INDEX